CRIMINAL APPEALS AND REVIEW REMEDIES FOR MAGISTRATES' COURT DECISIONS

Andrew William Keogh, LLB(Hons) Barrister
Solicitor of the Supreme Court
Higher Courts Advocate (Criminal Proceedings)

BLACKSTONE
PRESS LIMITED

First published in Great Britain 1999 by Blackstone Press Limited, Aldine Place, London W12 8AA. Telephone: 0181-740 2277

© Andrew Keogh, 1999

ISBN: 1 85431 973 6

British Library Cataloguing in Publication Data
A CIP catalogue record for this book is available from the British Library

Typeset by Montage Studios Limited, Horsmonden, Kent
Printed by Livesey Ltd, Shrewsbury, Shropshire

CRIN
REVI
MAC
DECI

Contents

Preface

This book is intended as a starting point for newly qualified solicitors and barristers, who cut their teeth in the magistrates' courts.

All available remedies are discussed, with an emphasis on combining commentary with relevant statutory materials and case law. Unlike some books which place legislation in appendices, wherever possible the rules are reproduced within the body of the text, so that the reader will become familiar with their intricacy. The legislative and case law provisions are supplemented by draft precedents.

The book does not provide the complete solution to appeal problems, and readers will need to consult the many specialist texts after identifying an appeal route.

It is hoped that this book will enable advocates to recognise at the outset of their career the fact that justice is not always achieved at the first port of call, and wit and determination is needed to protect a client's interests.

The magistrates' courts are imperfect places, with far too much emphasis on legally unqualified justices. That, combined in many cases with non-legally educated clerks, makes a recipe for a future miscarriage of justice.

I am grateful to those who have given permission to reproduce material, including the House of Lords and Legal Aid Board.

I wish to express my thanks to my wife, to whom this book is dedicated, for her support and patience, and to my parents for their devotion throughout my life.

The law is as stated on 10 February 1999.

Andrew Keogh
Wigan
February 1999

Table of Cases

Table of Statutes

1 Appeal and Review — an Overview

INTRODUCTION

The numerous remedies available in summary proceedings would no doubt come as a surprise to many people. One of the most difficult problems is to identify which remedy is appropriate and act accordingly. How often has one taken part in a trial in the magistrates' court, the client has been convicted and one has not even thought to advise on appeal? In addition to appealing the obvious issues of guilt and innocence or a particular sentence handed down, one must not forget the quasi-interlocutory activities of magistrates, such as bail, mode of trial, committal, amongst others.

All of these give rise to important issues, often affecting a defendant more than the ultimate trial of issue itself. What use is an independent witness if they will not come to trial and the magistrates will not issue a witness summons? What use is innocence if the defendant has served time in custody and lost his job as a result, due to an erroneous bail decision, or even one which is *ultra vires* (as happens all too often in the youth court)?

APPEAL OR REVIEW

There is an important distinction between appeal and review, and it is central to the use and availability of remedies. To appeal a decision is to reopen it afresh. A newly constituted tribunal hears the matter from scratch and reaches its own independent outcome.

To review does not mean to substitute, it is merely to examine *the way* in which a decision was reached as opposed to examining *the merits* of that decision. A tribunal which reviews can be said to have supervisory powers over another, inferior body.

The following table illustrates the options available:

DECISION	APPEAL?	REVIEW?
Conviction	To Crown Court By case stated	Yes, but should normally appeal first. If breach of natural justice then perhaps review appropriate
Sentence	To Crown Court By case stated (rarely — *judicial review* better remedy)	Yes — rare, appeal first
Bail	To Crown Court To High Court	Yes, but should appeal first
Mode of trial	No, not unless prosecution under customs and excise legislation	Yes
Committal	No	Yes
Bind over	To Crown Court	Yes, but appeal first
Witness summons	No	Yes
Submission of no case	By appealing the conviction	Yes
Abuse of process	By appealing the conviction	Yes
Breaches of natural justice	Appeal to Crown Court; however, this does not cure defect No case stated	Yes
New evidence following conviction	Appeal to Crown Court out of time Criminal cases review commission	Yes, but rarely appropriate
Other interlocutory rulings	No (unless specific statutory right) Case stated	Yes, exceptionally

MAKING THE CHOICE

When faced with a number of options it is necessary to examine much more closely the result which you are trying to achieve. Judicial review and case stated are all very well but, in reality, is your client going to come into the office and complete the legal aid forms? There is also a timescale to consider, which many defendants find unacceptable and that, coupled with the inability to assess prospects of success accurately, makes a Crown Court appeal all the more attractive to many.

The setting up of the Criminal Cases Review Commission, and the ability to reopen magistrates' court convictions and sentencing, has been one of the more positive steps in recent years. Legal Aid other than under the Advice and Assistance scheme is not available.

Anyone considering an appeal should start with the basics. Was the summons served? Could we reopen (remembering now that there is no 28 day limit)? Then thought must be given to Crown Court appeals and the availability of High Court remedies. At the same time, a practitioner must make sure that the victory is not only Pyrrhic. Is bail available pending appeal? Could a driving disqualification be suspended? The answers to all these questions are important to the client, and the answers can be found in this text.

It is time for practitioners to become much more aggressive and proactive in respect of our system of summary justice. The familiarity with the system of local justice very often has the effect of breeding a contempt for the finer points of justice. It would appear that it is only in the last five years or so that practitioners have become alert to the availability of challenges to interlocutory rulings, despite the importance of many of them. The challenges in 1998 alone to legal aid refusals were many, wielding positive results for the profession. It was the knowledge of the appeal and review systems which enabled these practitioners to advance their client's cause and make us all much more aware of the rights available.

2   Statutory Declarations

INTRODUCTION

A statutory declaration has the effect of making void a summons and all subsequent proceedings. The purpose of the procedure is to notify the court that the applicant has had no notice of the proceedings against him.

Where the grievance is lack of knowledge of the proceedings, the statutory declaration procedure should be adopted as opposed to seeking redress by way of judicial review (*Brighton Justices, ex parte Robinson* [1973] 1 WLR 69).

LEGAL BASIS

Section 14, Magistrates' Courts Act 1980, provides:

> 14(1)   Where a summons has been issued under section 1 above and a magistrates' court has begun to try the information to which the summons relates, then, if—
>
> (a)   the accused at any time during or after the trial, makes a statutory declaration that he did not know of the summons or the proceedings until a date specified in the declaration, being a date after the court has begun to try the information; and
>
> (b)   within 21 days of that date the declaration is served on the clerk to the justices, without prejudice to the validity of the information, the summons and all subsequent proceedings shall be void.
>
> (2)   [service of declaration]
>
> (3)   If on the application of the accused it appears to a magistrates' court (which for this purpose may be composed of a single justice) that it was not reasonable to expect the accused to serve such a statutory declaration as is mentioned in subsection (1) above within the period allowed by that subsection, the court may accept service of such a declaration by the accused after that period

has expired; and a statutory declaration accepted under this subsection shall be deemed to have been served as required by that subsection.

(4)   Where any proceedings have become void by virtue of subsection (1) above, the information shall not be tried again by the same justices.

APPLICATION

An application to swear a statutory declaration must be made within 21 days of the accused knowing of the proceedings against him. If 21 days have expired, it will be for the accused to show good reason as to why that period should be extended. The longer the period of delay, the greater the likelihood that the declaration will not be accepted. Justices should bear in mind the need to carry out a balancing exercise, considering also the inevitable damage to the Crown's case which results from delay.

A standard form of declaration is available free from any magistrates' court, and a copy precedent is reproduced at the end of this chapter. At the point the declaration is accepted the conviction or proceedings become a nullity, with any penalties thereunder having no effect. It is clear that unless the court has started to hear evidence on the trial of the matter, a declaration cannot be made.

A prosecutor may reissue process immediately in court if present, otherwise a summons will need to be reissued in the normal manner. The new summons, if it should disclose an offence triable summarily only, shall not be time-barred by reason of the previously annulled proceedings.

With the new relaxed section 142 reopenings it may be thought more expedient to use that avenue. However, a defence advocate should be alert to the possibility that the prosecution will not bother to reissue process, or that the reissuing will be lost within the ether of the file manager's office at the police station. There appears to be no good reason to assist the Crown in its pursuit of your client.

OFFENCE

A person who knowingly and willingly makes a false statement in a statutory declaration commits an offence under s. 5, Perjury Act 1911.

STATUTORY DECLARATIONS ACT 1835

I [NAME] OF [ADDRESS] do solemnly and sincerely declare that:

Until [DATE] I had no knowledge of the summons or proceedings against me, alleging an offence/offences of

[STATE OFFENCE(S)]

Alleged to have been committed on [DATE OF OFFENCE(S)]

And I make this solemn declaration conscientiously believing the same to be true, and by virtue of the provisions of the Statutory Declarations Act 1835.

[SIGNATURE OF ACCUSED MAKING DECLARATION]
Dated the [DATE]

Declared before me [SIGNATURE OF JUSTICE OF THE PEACE] or [SOLICITOR]
Justice of the Peace for the County of [COUNTY] or [SOLICITOR OF THE SUPREME COURT]

3 Magistrates' Power to Reopen a Case

INTRODUCTION

Section 142, Magistrates' Courts Act 1980, provides for the reopening of any order, determination, conviction or sentence, where it would be in the interests of justice to do so. The amended section came into effect on 1 January 1996, but applies retrospectively.

142. Power of magistrates' court to re-open cases to rectify mistakes etc.—

(1) A magistrates' court may vary or rescind a sentence or other order imposed or made by it when dealing with an offender if it appears to the court to be in the interests of justice to do so; and it is hereby declared that this power extends to replacing a sentence or order which for any reason appears to be invalid by another which the court has power to impose or make.

(1A) The power conferred on a magistrates' court by subsection (1) above shall not be exercisable in relation to any sentence or order imposed or made by it when dealing with an offender if—

(a) the Crown Court has determined an appeal against—

(i) that sentence or order;

(ii) the conviction in respect of which that sentence or order was imposed or made; or

(iii) any other sentence or order imposed or made by the magistrates' court when dealing with the offender in respect of that conviction (including a sentence or order replaced by that sentence or order); or

(b) the High Court has determined a case stated for the opinion of that court on any question arising in any proceeding leading to or resulting from the imposition or making of the sentence or order.

(2) Where a person is convicted by a magistrates' court and it subsequently appears to the court that it would be in the interests of justice that the case should be heard again by different justices, the court may so direct.

(2A)   The power conferred on a magistrates' court by subsection (2) above shall not be exercisable in relation to a conviction if—

(a)   the Crown Court has determined an appeal against—

(i)   the conviction; or

(ii)   any sentence or order imposed or made by the magistrates' court when dealing with the offender in respect of the conviction; or

(b)   the High Court has determined a case stated for the opinion of that court on any question arising in any proceeding leading to or resulting from the conviction.

(3)   Where a court gives a direction under subsection (2) above—

(a)   the conviction and any sentence or other order imposed or made in consequence thereof shall be of no effect; and

(b)   section 10(4) above shall apply as if the trial of the person in question had been adjourned.

(4)   *Repealed.*

(5)   Where a sentence or order is varied under subsection (1) above, the sentence or other order, as so varied, shall take effect from the beginning of the day on which it was originally imposed or made, unless the court otherwise directs.

[Magistrates' Courts Act 1980, s. 142 as amended by the Criminal Appeal Act 1995, s. 26 and Sch. 3.]

PROCEDURE

The application can be made orally or in writing, there is no requirement for the applicant to be present. The power is open to the Crown or other prosecuting agency, a private prosecutor or defendant, and the opposing party in the proceedings should be afforded an opportunity to make representations.

It is clear that the applicant should not attempt to overturn a conviction or sentence merely because it was dissatisfied with the outcome. Whilst a convicted applicant with new evidence may (exceptionally) have grounds for an application to reopen, it is clear that the Crown in a similar position could not seek to reopen an acquittal, as this offends against the double jeopardy rule.

An applicant who has previously appealed to the Crown Court, or has applied to state a case, cannot later attempt to have a matter reopened (s. 142(1A) and (2A)). An application could, however, be made to the Criminal Cases Review Commission.

The purpose of s. 142 is to enable the court to rectify mistakes, and is to be regarded as a slip rule. Accordingly, s. 142 has no application where there has been an unequivocal guilty plea (*Croydon Youth Court, ex parte Director of Public Prosecutions* [1997] 2 Cr App R 411, DC).

The Court should not generally allow a reopening because there has been a change in the law, as such a reopening offends against having a certainty of justice.

TIME LIMITS

The effect of the Criminal Appeal Act 1995 was to remove the previous 28 day time limit. However, the timeliness of the application is one factor to be considered (although it is not determinative), and the former 28 day limit should be regarded as a salutary guideline (*Ealing Magistrates' Court, ex parte Sahota* (1997) *The Times*, 9 December 1997).

Considerations

The concept of 'interests of justice' (s. 142(1)) is wide and undefinable. A court must consider all the surrounding circumstances, including:

- why the convicted person did not appear at the original trial (if the application relates to the reopening of the conviction);
- timeliness of application;
- reason (if any) for delay in making the application;
- importance of decision being questioned;
- inconvenience caused to the opposing party (for example, the fact that the Crown would now need to recall witnesses to give evidence for the second time);
- whether a more appropriate venue of appeal may be open to the applicant, including an appeal to the Crown Court, or judicial review. It may well be tempting for a court to reopen a conviction where a judicial review application is threatened, say on the grounds of procedural impropriety or bias. Care should be taken to evaluate any evidence put forward before acceding to such an application.

Justices are given a very wide discretion in determining what are relevant factors (*Gwent Magistrates' Court, ex parte Carey* (1996) 160 JP 613). They must, however, act judicially, and the fact for example that a defendant had arrived late at court has been held not to be a proper ground for refusing a rehearing (*Camberwell Green Magistrates' Court, ex parte Ibrahim* (1984) 148 JP 400).

EFFECTS OF REOPENING

In respect of a conviction the reopening has the effect of completely setting aside the conviction and any sentence or other order made. The matter is then treated as if it had been adjourned prior to trial.

The new trial must be heard before different justices from those (a) hearing the reopening and those (b) who sat during the original trial.

In respect of orders other than conviction, the court may vary or rescind the original finding, with the power extending to the replacing of a sentence or order, which for any reason appears invalid, with any other lawful order. A sentence or order varied takes effect from the date on which the original order was imposed, unless the court directs otherwise. A court may increase an order, but must take care not to offend against any legitimate expectation given to the offender (*Jane* v *Broome, The Times*, 2 November 1988).

CONCLUSION

The power to reopen cases is a powerful tool of summary justice and it is important that practitioners do not ignore it. In appropriate cases, with well argued submissions, the expense of Crown Court appeals can be avoided. Section 142 is not however a mechanism for continuing to argue the merits of a case which has previously been rejected — that remains the province of the Crown Court, where appeals against conviction and sentence lie as of right.

Set out below is a standard form of letter for the reopening of a magistrates' court finding:

Marston and Co. Solicitors

13 Old Bank Road, Newfield, Newtown

Clerk to the Justices
Manor Magistrates' Court
Old Town Lane
Newtown
NT1 1AS

15 July 1998

Dear Sirs,

We are instructed on behalf of John Arnold Cooper, born 10.1.79, of 13 Luck Street, Newtown. Mister Cooper was convicted in his absence on 10 June 1998 in respect of a matter of criminal damage, on the same date a fine of £200 was imposed with costs of £100 and compensation of £12.84. Unfortunately, he did not attend for trial on the date in question due to the death a week earlier of his mother. Somewhat understandably the imminent court hearing was at the back of his mind. In all the circumstances I would ask that this information be put before the court at the earliest opportunity and ask that the conviction and sentence be set aside. My client maintains his innocence and has witnesses to call in his defence, additionally the fine and costs imposed are clearly beyond the means of our client. At the present time Mister Cooper is not legally aided and we would ask that our attendance at this stage be excused. However, if we can provide any further information then please do not hesitate to contact this office.

Yours faithfully,

Marston and Co. Solicitors

4   Crown Court Rules and Procedure

INTRODUCTION

Many decisions of the magistrates' court are appealable to the Crown Court. Besides the usual well-known right of appeal against conviction and sentence, other matters including bail, exclusion orders, custody time limits and bind overs are appealable. The Crown Court provides a quick, simple and relatively inexpensive system of appeal, with the appellant being afforded a rehearing. The rules, procedures and powers exercisable on such appeals are largely similar, save in bail cases; this chapter details those rules and procedures, any variations being dealt with in their appropriate chapters. A youth court, for the purposes of appeal, is treated as if it were a magistrates' court and accordingly the same rules apply.

THE CROWN COURT RULES

These rules (SI 1982/1109), with subsequent amendments, provide the broad framework within which the practitioner must both work and find familiarity. The rules need to be read in conjunction with the many Divisional Court decisions concerning appeal procedures.

Rule 6 provides:

> (1)   Subject to the following provisions of this Rule, this Part of these Rules shall apply to every appeal which by or under any enactment lies to the Crown Court from any court, tribunal or person except any appeal against a decision of a magistrates' court under section 22(7) or (8) of the Prosecution of Offences Act 1985 or under section 1 of the Bail (Amendment) Act 1993.

It can be seen that the rules themselves do not provide the actual avenue of appeal, the rules simply state that they apply to every appeal which by or under any other enactment lies to the Crown Court. Rule 6 expressly mentions two appeal procedures that fall outside these rules, namely in relation to custody time limits and prosecution appeals against the grant of bail.

COMMENCING THE APPEAL PROCESS

Appeals are commenced by the giving of a notice of appeal (r. 7(1)), which must be in writing (r. 7(2)). A copy of the notice of appeal must be served upon the clerk to the magistrates' court (r. 7(2)(a)) and any other party to the appeal (r. 7(2)(e)). Generally the other party to the appeal will be the Crown Prosecution Service. However, it should be noted that a private prosecutor must be served with notice of appeal. Service need not be by post and is generally effected by handing the completed notice to the prosecutor and clerk at court.

FORM OF NOTICE

A sample notice of appeal is set out at the end of this chapter. Proforma notices are available free of charge from all magistrates' courts.

The notice must state whether the appeal is against conviction or sentence or both (r. 7(4)(a)). No grounds of appeal need be given; however, as a matter of courtesy it is generally stated that the appeal is due to the 'conviction being against the weight of the evidence' or that the 'sentence is excessive'. Keeping comments to the minimum is advisable as the judge will have a copy of the notice, and any inconsistent defence put forward later may act upon the court's mind. In cases where the appeal is on a point of law alone, citing authorities is helpful, though not necessary.

TIME LIMITS

The notice must be served within 21 days of the decision being appealed against having been given. The following exceptions apply:

● In the case of a trial adjourned after conviction, the notice need only be served within 21 days of final disposal of the case (i.e. sentence).
● Practitioners will note that this differs from the position with appeals from the Crown Court to the Court of Appeal.
● In the case of a deferred sentence, the operative date is the date on which the deferment was made (r. 7(3)).
● In respect of appeals against the forfeiture of cash under s. 43, Drug Trafficking Act 1994, an appellant has 30 days in which to appeal (s. 44, DTA 1994).

Extension of Time Limits

In the event of the 21 days having expired, an extension of time will need to be applied for. In the case where an appellant is also seeking judicial review of the decision being appealed, it is preferable still to lodge the appeal within the 21 days with a note detailing the fact of a judicial review. This should be enough to stop the Crown Court appeal being listed before the High Court determination. In the event that the Crown Court insists on proceeding before the High Court application has been heard, a stay of proceedings will need to be applied for.

An application for extension of time can be made either before or after expiry of the relevant period (r. 7(5)). Applications must be made in writing to the appropriate officer of the Crown Court (generally the senior clerk) and must state the grounds for such an application (r. 7(6)).

In considering an application for extension of time, the court may take into account the merits of the case, there is no right to an oral argument and the judge need not give reasons for the decision to refuse leave to appeal out of time (*Croydon Crown Court, ex parte Smith* (1983) 77 Cr App R 277, DC).

If an extension is given, notice of that extension will be served upon the appellant and clerk to the magistrates' court. It is then the duty of the appellant to serve the notice of extension upon the other party to the appeal (r. 7(7)).

It would appear that there is no obligation to notify the opposing party of the fact that an extension is being applied for. However, in *Director of Public Prosecutions v Coleman, The Times*, 13 December 1997, DC, an obligation to make an inter partes application was imported into r. 23 (which deals with procedure in respect of the stating of a case). It would appear that the rationale behind the ruling was the fact that the prosecution were seeking to extend a time period, putting the review of the respondent's acquittal in further jeopardy. Arguably the Crown are entitled to the same consideration.

NOTICE OF HEARING

It is the duty of the Crown Court to enter the appeal and give notice of hearing to the appellant, clerk to the magistrates' court and any other party to the appeal (r. 8). It is important that a proper record is kept of service, since in the event of the appellant's non-appearance at the appeal it will need to be shown that the notice of hearing was properly served if the court intends to dismiss the appeal.

ABANDONMENT OF APPEAL

This can occur in two instances:

● Section 111(4), Magistrates' Courts Act 1980 states that all rights of appeal to the Crown Court shall cease upon the appellant applying to the High Court for the case to be stated.
● Rule 11 of the Crown Court Rules lays down the procedure for abandonment of an appeal by the appellant. Notice of abandonment is required at least three days before the appeal is due to be heard. Provided that the notice of abandonment is received within this time an appellant may abandon as of right. Notice of

abandonment, which need not be in any particular form, should be served upon the Crown Court, magistrates' court and the other party to the appeal (r. 11(2)).

In the event, as frequently happens, that the appellant receives advice on the day of the appeal to abandon, leave must be sought from the court. It should only be in exceptional circumstances that a judge would *refuse* leave to abandon if the request were made before the hearing had begun, or *allow* leave after it had begun (*Manchester Crown Court, ex parte Welby* (1981) 73 Cr App R 248, DC).

Effect of Abandonment

There is no provision for reinstatement once an appeal has been abandoned. In the case where an abandonment can be deemed a nullity through mistake or fraudulent inducement, the Crown Court may entertain a further appeal. The court should, however, take particular care in establishing that the circumstances alleged are genuine (*Essex QS Appeals Committee, ex parte Larkin* [1962] 1 QB 712).

If the court allows abandonment of an appeal, it has no power then to review the sentence: such power is only open to the court on 'the termination of the hearing of the appeal' (*Gloucester Crown Court, ex parte Betteridge, The Times*, 4 August 1997, DC).

Once an appeal has been abandoned, the magistrates' court may (and indeed should) issue process to enforce its original decision (s. 109, Magistrates' Courts Act 1980). Section 109 further allows the respondent to recover costs incurred before the abandonment notice was given:

109(1) Where notice to abandon an appeal has been duly given by the appellant—

(a) the court against whose decision the appeal was brought may issue process for enforcing that decision, subject to anything already suffered or done under it by the appellant; and

(b) the said court may, on the application of the other party to the appeal, order the appellant to pay to that party such costs as appear to the court to be just and reasonable in respect of expenses properly incurred by that party in connection with the appeal before notice of the abandonment was given to that party.

(2) In this section 'appeal' means an appeal from a magistrates' court to the Crown Court, and the reference to a notice to abandon an appeal is a reference to a notice shown to the satisfaction of the magistrates' court to have been given in accordance with Crown Court rules.

ATTENDANCE OF PARTIES AND EFFECT OF ABSENCE

● An appellant is entitled to appear in person at the appeal. Any denial of the appellant's right to address the court would amount to a denial of natural justice.

• If both parties fail to attend and neither is represented by counsel, the appeal should be dismissed (*Guildford Crown Court, ex parte Brewer* (1988) 87 Cr App R 265, DC).
• The appellant need not attend the appeal if an advocate has been instructed to appear on the appellant's behalf; the tradition of asking for leave to continue in the appellant's absence is a mere courtesy to the court (s. 122, Magistrates' Courts Act 1980). In such circumstances the court cannot dismiss the appeal without first hearing evidence (*Podmore* v *DPP* [1997] COD 80, DC). If the advocate appearing has no instructions the appeal should continue, the advocate's duty being to put the crown to proof (*ex parte Brewer, ante*).

If neither the appellant nor someone instructed on his behalf appears, the court has the following options, the first being the more likely to be followed:

• If the notice of hearing is proved to have been served then the court can dismiss the appeal (*Croydon Crown Court, ex parte Clair* [1986] 2 All ER 716).
• The court can adjourn the appeal, allowing the appellant a further chance to appear.
• The court can continue to hear the appeal. This option may be followed in the case where the court recognised a very weak case, particularly with an evidential flaw identified in the notice of appeal. It is submitted that this kind of case and exercise of judicial fairness would be rare indeed.

If the respondent fails to appear, the court may either adjourn the matter or (provided proof of notice of appeal is in order) allow the appellant's appeal (*ex parte Clair, ante*). It is not proper for the judge to conduct the appeal on the respondent's behalf (*Wood Green Crown Court, ex parte Taylor* [1995] Crim LR 879).

The appeal will lapse if the appellant dies (*Jefferies* (1968) 52 Cr App R 654, CA).

SUSPENSION OF ORDERS AND SENTENCES PENDING APPEAL

In general orders and sentences are not stayed pending an appeal. An appellant ordered to complete community service, for example, must report to the appropriate body and abide by their instructions pending the determination of the appeal, such breaches being punishable even if the sentence is not upheld on appeal. Individual provisions apply in respect of compensation orders, custodial sentences and an order of disqualification from driving. It is, however, the practice of magistrates' courts not to enforce fines before the time for appeal has expired and, in the event of an appeal, not until its final determination.

Compensation orders do not take effect until after the expiry of the time allowed for appeal or until after the determination of an appeal if one is entered (s. 36, Powers of Criminal Courts Act 1973).

It will be no defence to a charge of driving whilst disqualified to show that the disqualification was not upheld on appeal; until such time as an order of disqualification is quashed, it is a lawful order of the court and must be obeyed (*Thames Magistrates' Court, ex parte Levy, The Times*, 17 July 1997, DC).

BAIL PENDING APPEAL

Since custodial sentences imposed by magistrates' courts tend in many cases to be short, the punishment can often be completed before an appeal is heard. Accordingly, advisers need to be fully aware of the provisions relating to bail pending appeal. An appellant may apply to the magistrates' court, Crown Court or High Court for bail.

●   Section 113, Magistrates' Courts Act 1980 provides for the grant of bail pending appeal (subject to s. 25, Criminal Justice and Public Order Act 1994) where notice of appeal has been given. Any bail granted is until the notice of hearing of the appeal, with the court having power to impose conditions of bail in the normal way.
●   Similarly, the Crown Court has the right to grant bail pending appeal. Typically the preferred option is to expedite the appeal hearing rather than give bail.
●   A further avenue open to the appellant is the High Court. If the magistrates' court has given conditional bail, and the appellant seeks variation pending the appeal, then the only challenge to those conditions is by way of appeal to the High Court.

The detailed provisions relating to bail appeals can be found in the chapter on bail. It should be noted that bail pending appeal is rarely granted and the appellant should carefully consider whether in the event of bail being granted his appeal is likely to succeed — a return to custody may be more traumatic than the initial spell. The Court of Appeal in the case of an appeal from the Crown Court, where the appellant was granted bail pending appeal and the custodial sentence was upheld, commented that appellants know the risk of being returned to prison; the previous granting of bail pending appeal was not in itself a reason for allowing the appeal (*Partington* Transcript No 96/3718/x5).

SUSPENSION OF DRIVING DISQUALIFICATION

Any appellant who has been disqualified from driving, whether due to discretionary or mandatory provisions of disqualification, can apply to the magistrates' court (s. 39, Road Traffic Offenders Act 1988) or Crown Court (s. 40, RTOA 1988) for that disqualification to be suspended pending appeal:

39(1)   Any court in England and Wales (whether a magistrates' court or another) which makes an order disqualifying a person may, if it thinks fit, suspend the disqualification pending an appeal against the order.
(2)   [not relevant]
(3)   Where a court exercises its power under subsection (1) . . . above, it must send notice of the suspension to the Secretary of State.

(4)   The notice must be sent in such manner and to such address and must contain such particulars as the Secretary of State may determine.

40(1)   This section applies where a person has been convicted by or before a court in England and Wales of an offence involving obligatory or discretionary disqualification and has been ordered to be disqualified; and in the following provisions of this section—

(a)   any reference to a person ordered to be disqualified is to be construed as a reference to a person so convicted and so ordered to be disqualified, and

(b)   any reference to his sentence includes a reference to the order of disqualification and to any other order made on his conviction and, accordingly, any reference to an appeal against his sentence includes a reference to an appeal against any order forming part of his sentence.

(2)   Where a person ordered to be disqualified—

(a)   appeals to the Crown Court, or

(b)   appeals or applies for leave to appeal to the Court of Appeal,

against his conviction or his sentence, the Crown Court or, as the case may require, the Court of Appeal may, if it thinks fit, suspend the disqualification.

The procedure is generally to make an oral application at the time of lodging the notice of appeal with the magistrates' court. In practice it will be rare that an appellant needs to make such an application to the Crown Court, but may do so if the magistrates' court does not allow the application.

ROAD TRAFFIC (NEW DRIVERS) ACT 1995 — LICENCE REVOCATION

Provision is made under the New Drivers (Appeals Procedure) Regulations 1997 (SI 1997/1098) to allow an appellant with a revoked licence to drive, pending an appeal determination. Driving is allowed by virtue of the issue of a new licence (or test certificate), provided the following conditions are satisfied:

● A previous licence or test certificate must have been revoked (it should be noted that due to the fact that revocation does not take place until the convicted person is notified in writing, the appeal may well be heard before a licence is revoked and therefore these procedures may not be necessary).

● The Secretary of State must have received notice of the appeal, from the magistrates' court or Crown Court, or in the event of case stated from the High Court (or Crown Court if it is that court which has been asked to state a case). Notice should be served as soon as reasonably practicable.

● The appellant's licence or test certificate must have been previously surrendered, or an explanation considered adequate by the Secretary of State must be provided.

● The new licence is valid for a period expiring on the date the previous licence would have expired, had it not been revoked.

• The new licence will be revoked if, following the appeal, the penalty points taken into account for the purposes of s. 2(1) of the Road Traffic (New Drivers) Act 1995, are not reduced to a smaller number than six, or the appeal is abandoned. Notice of abandonment of appeal must be given to the Secretary of State by the appellate court.

THE APPEAL HEARING

Provision of Notes of Evidence

In cases where legal aid is granted, both appellant and respondent are entitled to a copy of the clerk's notes of evidence:

Legal Aid in Criminal and Care Proceedings (General) Regulations 1989 reg. 42, SI 1989/344

> Where a legal aid order is made in respect of an appeal to the Crown Court, the justices' clerk shall supply, on the application of the solicitor assigned to the appellant or respondent on whose application such an order was made, copies of any notes of evidence or depositions taken in the proceedings in the magistrates' court.

In non-legal aid cases there is no requirement to provide the notes; however, it was observed in *Highbury Corner Justices, ex parte Hussein* (1987) 84 Cr App R 112, DC, that there should be no disadvantage to non-legally aided appellants and any request for notes should be dealt with sympathetically. Despite more forthright views supporting an absolute right it is submitted that this case now represents the law.

Appearance of Justices

The justices have a right to appear in the Crown Court upon the hearing of an appeal. In such a situation it is desirable to instruct counsel. The justices' role is not to challenge or cross-examine witnesses but simply to explain their decision if they think it appropriate. It is submitted that particularly in sentencing appeals, greater use should be made of this opportunity, as the justices then have an opportunity to explain any particular rationale behind the sentence, for example the prevalence of a particular offence in the locality.

Adjourning Proceedings

The rules contain no provisions in relation to adjournments. Section 10(3), Magistrates' Courts Act 1980 (which allows for adjournments of three weeks if a party is in custody, four weeks otherwise), should be taken as applying to the Crown Court in its appellate capacity (*Arthur* v *Stringer* (1987) 84 Cr App R 361, DC).

Composition of Court on Appeal

Section 74, Supreme Court Act 1981 (SCA 1981) regulates the composition of the court. The court is to consist of a judge of the High Court or a circuit judge or a recorder, sitting with not less than two nor more than four justices. Typically no more than two justices will sit. In the case of an appeal from the youth court, each justice must be a member of the youth panel, and the bench must have both a man and a woman.

Any objection to the composition of the court must be made either before the hearing or at the point when the irregularity began, no appeal hearing can be challenged later if this is not done (s. 74(6), SCA 1981).

A court so notified of an irregularity cannot begin to hear the appeal if the court is indeed improperly composed. However, if the irregularity occurs once the hearing has started, for instance a justice withdraws through illness, the court has a discretion to continue to hear the appeal (r. 4(3)).

In addition r. 4(1) allows the court to sit with only one justice (who in the case of an appeal from the youth court must be a member of the youth panel) if it appears to the judge that the court could not otherwise be constituted without unreasonable delay. Whilst the decision is one for the judge it is right that any advocate faced with this submission should voice objections and seek to persuade the court to adjourn.

In respect of appeals against conviction and sentence there is no provision for agreeing to waive the presence of justices (unlike in licensing matters for example). It is submitted that such a practice would be highly undesirable in any event.

Disqualification of Justices

Rule 5 states that a justice of the peace must not sit in the Crown Court on the hearing of an appeal in a matter on which he adjudicated. It is vital that the court avoids any appearance of bias, any connection or interest in the matter should be declared to the parties to the appeal so that they can make representations (*Bristol Crown Court, ex parte Cooper* [1989] 1 WLR 878, DC).

Adjudications

The judge presides at the appeal, decisions being taken by majority. In the event of an even split the judge retains a further casting vote (s. 73(3), SCA 1981). Justices must take part in all decision making including, for example, requests to adjourn, but they must take the judge's advice on matters of law.

It is important that the judge when announcing the decision of the court states that the justices have been consulted (*Newby* (1984) 6 Cr App R (S) 148, CA). The court should give reasons for its decisions, the detail of those reasons varying with the decision having been taken and the issues involved. Failure to give reasons may well equate to a denial of natural justice (*Harrow Crown Court, ex parte Dave* (1994) 99 Cr App R 114, DC).

CONCLUSION

Appeals to the Crown Court often involve complex issues of procedure. It can be seen that the bare bones provided by the Crown Court Rules have been greatly added to by many decisions of the Divisional Court, either by way of judicial review of Crown Court decisions or by case stated. It is important to remember that denial of a fair appeal may well open up a further challenge by way of review.

NOTICE OF APPEAL

To the Clerk of the Bow Street Magistrates' Court, in the Inner London Area

And To:
Mr Jonathan Knight, Branch Crown Prosecutor, of 13 Dimble Street, London SW1A.

I, Mark James Lemon, of 1 King Street, Lewisham, Hereby notify you that it is my intention to appeal to the Crown Court sitting at Harrow, against a conviction of me by the Bow Street Magistrates' Court in the Inner London Area, on the 1st Day of July 1998, for having on the 3rd May 1998 Assaulted Jamie Lemon, contrary to section 39 Criminal Justice Act 1988.
The finding of guilt was against the weight of the evidence, and I am not guilty of the said offence.

Dated:

Signed:

STATUTORY INSTRUMENTS

1997 No. 1098

ROAD TRAFFIC

The New Drivers (Appeals Procedure) Regulations 1997

Made	*26th March 1997*
Laid before Parliament	*1st April 1997*
Coming into force	*1st June 1997*

The Secretary of State for Transport, in exercise of the powers conferred by section 5 of, and paragraph 11 of Schedule 1 to, the Road Traffic (New Drivers) Act 1995, hereby makes the following Regulations:—

Citation, commencement and interpretation

1.—(1)   These Regulations may be cited as the New Drivers (Appeals Procedure) Regulations 1997 and shall come into force on 1st June 1997.

(2)   In these Regulations—

'the Act' means the Road Traffic (New Drivers) Act 1995;
'appellate court' means—

(a)   in England and Wales, the Crown Court, the High Court or the Court of Appeal, as the case may be;

(b)   in Scotland, the High Court of Justiciary;

'relevant appeal' means an appeal against—

(a)   a conviction, or

(b)   an order of a court in England and Wales for the endorsement of a licence or a sentence passed by a court in Scotland which includes an order for the endorsement of a licence,

which is, or forms part of, the basis for the revocation of the licence or a test certificate.

Licences granted pending appeal

2.—(1)   There is prescribed for the purposes of section 5(1) of the Act (duration of licences granted without retesting pending appeal) a period expiring on the date on which the revoked licence would have expired if it had not been revoked.

(2)   Where the Secretary of State has—

(a)   revoked a person's test certificate under paragraph 5(1) of Schedule 1 to the Act or, as the case may be, revoked a person's licence and test certificate under paragraph 8(1) of that Schedule, and

(b)   received notice that the person is making a relevant appeal,

he must, if that person surrenders to him any previous licence granted to him or provides an explanation for not surrendering it that the Secretary of State considers adequate, grant to that person a full licence in accordance with paragraph (3) below.

(3)   A licence granted under paragraph (2) above shall—

(a)   have effect for the purposes of the Road Traffic Acts as if it were a licence granted under Part III of the Road Traffic Act 1988,

(b)   subject to section 92 and Part IV of that Act, authorise the driving of all classes of vehicle which, immediately before his test certificate was revoked, the person was permitted to drive without observing the prescribed conditions, and

(c)   subject to paragraph (4) below, be for a period expiring on the date on which a licence granted under Part III of that Act would have expired.

(4)   A licence granted under paragraph (2) shall be treated as revoked if—

(a)   following the appeal, the penalty points taken into account for the purposes of section 2(1) of the Act are not reduced to a number smaller than six, or

(b)   the appeal is abandoned.

Notices of appeal

3.—(1)   Subject to paragraphs (2) and (3) below, notice of a relevant appeal shall be given to the Secretary of State—

(a)   in England and Wales, by the magistrates' court or Crown Court in which the case is heard;

(b)   in Scotland, by the Sheriff Court or district court in which the case is heard.

(2)   Notice of a relevant appeal from a magistrates' court or Crown Court by case stated shall be given to the Secretary of State by the High Court.

(3)   Notice of a further appeal from a decision of an appellate court shall be given to the Secretary of State by the appellate court from which the appeal is made.

(4)   A notice pursuant to this regulation shall be given—

(a)   in the case of an appeal by case stated, as soon as reasonably practicable after the day on which the case is lodged in the High Court;

(b)   in the case of any other appeal—

(i)   where leave to appeal or for abridgement of time is necessary, as soon as reasonably practicable after the court has granted such leave or abridgement, or

(ii)   in any other case, as soon as reasonably practicable after notice of appeal is duly given by the appellant.

Notice of abandonment of appeal

4.   Notice of the abandonment of any relevant appeal shall be given to the Secretary of State—

(a)   in England and Wales, by the appellate court to which the appeal is made, or

(b)   in Scotland, by the Sheriff Court or district court in which the case is heard, as soon as reasonably practicable after the day on which notice of the abandonment of the appeal is duly given.

Signed by authority of the Secretary of State for Transport

John Bowis
Parliamentary Under Secretary of State, Department of Transport

26th March 1997

EXPLANATORY NOTE

(This note is not part of the Regulations)

These Regulations make provision in respect of the procedure to be followed when a person whose licence or test certificate has been revoked by the Secretary of State under the Road Traffic (New Drivers) Act 1995 appeals against his conviction or the terms of the licence endorsement order made by the court.

They specify the nature and duration of a licence granted by the Secretary of State pending determination of the appeal and prescribe which court must give to the Secretary of State notice of the appeal and of any subsequent abandonment thereof.

5   Appeals against Conviction and Sentence

BASIC CONCEPTS

Appeals can be against conviction and sentence, or merely against sentence alone. It is not open to an appellant to challenge just the conviction, and if unsuccessful accept the original sentence. The danger here is that in the case of appeals against sentence alone, sentence is at large and may be increased or varied. This situation arises as a result of s. 48(1), Supreme Court Act 1981 which is reproduced in full at the end of this chapter and referred to throughout it.

One exception to this rule is in respect of magistrates' court convictions which have been referred to the court by the Criminal Cases Review Commission. Section 11(6), Criminal Appeal Act 1995, provides:

> On a reference under this section the Crown Court may not award any punishment more severe than that awarded by the court whose decision is referred.

APPEALS AGAINST CONVICTION (WITH SENTENCE AT LARGE)

An appeal against conviction cannot be made where the appellant had originally pleaded guilty to the offence in the magistrates' court. Special rules apply in respect of appeals referred by the Criminal Cases Review Commission (see Chapter 13).

Equivocal and other Unsatisfactory Pleas

In limited circumstances the Crown Court can hear argument as to whether the guilty plea entered in the magistrates' court was equivocal. The appellant will need to show that some qualification was added to the guilty plea which might show that the appellant was not really admitting any guilt. A plea such as 'I am guilty but I acted in self-defence' is one such example. Alternatively the equivocality might be raised at a later stage, for example during mitigation or contained in a pre-sentence report. A plea entered under duress is not a valid plea, and the Crown Court has the power to act in such circumstances (*Huntingdon Crown Court, ex parte Jordan* [1981] QB 857).

Finally, it is open to an appellant to raise autrefois acquit or convict (*Cooper* v *New Forest DC* [1992] Crim LR 877).

A court will not grant relief where pleas are entered by mistake or because of a misapprehension on the part of the appellant.

A somewhat different situation arises where a person pleads guilty and is committed for sentence. Following *Inner London Crown Court, ex parte Sloper* (1979) 69 Cr App R 1, it would appear that the Crown Court has a discretion to remit the matter to the magistrates' court, where it appears just to do so. The point here is a jurisdictional one: the magistrates are still seized of the case, and are able therefore to entertain further argument from the accused as to the validity of the plea. Indeed if the Crown Court directs that a not guilty plea be entered, the lower court is not entitled to reject that plea.

Arguing Equivocality

The Crown Court must resolve the matter as a preliminary issue, after hearing evidence as to what was said and done before the lower court. Increasingly, solicitors' contemporaneous notes are becoming invaluable in cases of this kind (although one would hope in such cases that the situation would be immediately spotted). The judge should generally invite the justices and court clerk to submit affidavits as to their recollection. Solicitors are advised to do the same, any conflict being resolved in favour of the appellant.

If the court is persuaded that the plea was equivocal or that, for some other reason, it should be set aside, the case should be remitted to the magistrates for rehearing.

Provided the Crown Court has carried out due enquiry the magistrates must allow a not guilty plea to stand and the matter should be adjourned to trial (*Plymouth Justices, ex parte Hart* [1986] QB 950).

In the event of the magistrates' court refusing to hear the case, the matter would need to be resolved by the Divisional Court by way of mandamus.

FORMAT OF APPEAL

The appeal is heard *de novo*, with both the prosecution and defence presenting their cases according to the usual rules of evidence. In effect it is simply the magistrates' court trial all over again (SCA 1981, s. 79(3)).

Basis of Case

It is open to the Crown to present their case in a different way from the way in which it was presented before the magistrates' court, and open to the Crown Court to find the case proved on a different basis from that found by the court below (*Hingley-Smith* v *DPP* [1998] 1 Archbold News 2, DC). This includes calling evidence which was not presented at the magistrates' court.

Amendments to Charge

It is not open to the Crown Court to amend the information on which the appellant was originally convicted (see for example *Norwich Crown Court, ex parte Russell* [1993] Crim LR 518). This includes the reversal of an amendment made in the lower court.

However, the distinction can sometimes be a fine one. It is now clear law that the Crown Court can amend a defect if, had the lower court noticed it, it could have cured the defect by utilising s. 123, Magistrates' Courts Act 1980 (*Swansea Crown Court, ex parte Stacey* [1990] RTR 183). In the *Norwich Crown Court* decision, for example, the amendment of the date of the alleged offence was held to have been improper. The more recent decision in *Jevons* v *Cosmosair plc*, 161 JPN 173, DC appears to indicate that justices, and therefore the Crown Court on appeal, should take a more liberal view of the allowing of amendments by virtue of s. 123.

An excellent and detailed analysis of s. 123, Magistrates' Courts Act 1980 can be found in *Blackstone's Criminal Practice* 1998 at para. D19.7.

DECISIONS

The court has the power to allow or dismiss the appeal, in whole or in part. In doing so the court should give reasons, stating the contentious issues and how it resolved them. A failure to give reasons may, but not necessarily, amount to a breach of the rules of natural justice (*Harrow Crown Court, ex parte Dave* (1994) 99 Cr App R 114, DC).

Following a successful appeal, in whole or part, the court has the usual powers to make a defendant's costs order in appropriate cases.

If the appeal is dismissed the court will proceed to sentence in the usual way. Sentence is at large, and the principles in respect of the court's powers are discussed below.

APPEALS AGAINST SENTENCE

Section 108(3), Magistrates' Courts Act 1980 provides that 'sentence' includes any order made on conviction by a magistrates' court, except an order for the payment of costs, or an order for the destruction of an animal under s. 2 of the Protection of Animals Act 1911. 'Sentence' does not include an order made in pursuance of any enactment under which the court has no discretion as to the making of the order or its terms.

A challenge to a costs order should be made by way of judicial review (*Tottenham Justices, ex parte Joshi* (1982) 146 JP 268).

Committals for trial or sentence (*London Sessions, ex parte Rogers* [1951] 2 KB 74) are not made on conviction and accordingly cannot be challenged in this way. The appropriate remedy is judicial review.

Specific statutory authority allows appeals against recommendations for deportation (Immigration Act 1971, s. 6(5)(a)), and against guardianship orders under the Mental Health Act (Mental Health Act 1983, s. 70).

Because a mandatory disqualification would ordinarily be exempt from such an appeal, the Road Traffic Act 1972, s. 94(1), makes provision for such an appeal.

Other Rights of Appeal in Respect of a Sentence or Order

● Defendant sentenced for offence which had previously been dealt with by way of conditional discharge (MCA 1980, s. 108(2)).
● Defendant sentenced for breach of a community order, or attendance centre order.
● Defendant bound over (dealt with separately in this book).
● Parent or guardian ordered to pay fine, compensation or costs in respect of a youth.
● Defendant sentenced for contempt.
● Party aggrieved by the forfeiture of cash.

FORMAT OF THE APPEAL

The Supreme Court Act 1981, s. 79(3) provides:

> The customary practice and procedure with respect to appeals to the Crown Court and in particular any practice as to the extent to which an appeal is by way of rehearing of the case, shall continue to be observed.

In essence therefore, the procedure is as it would be in the magistrates' court, with the prosecution outlining the facts and any antecedents, and the appellant mitigating.

DISPOSALS

Except in the case of an appeal against conviction which is fully allowed, the question of disposal on sentence always arises. This fact is lost on many advocates, i.e. that sentence is at large even when the appellant is only aggrieved in respect of the conviction (note the exception in respect of referrals by the Criminal Cases Review Commission referred to at the start of this chapter).

The court should not have regard to the sentence imposed by the magistrates' court, but most advocates will be aware that this is one of the first enquiries the court will generally make. The court, having decided sentence afresh, should then compare it with the sentence passed below, and only if the difference is significant should the sentence be varied to that extent (either up or down).

The Crown Court must make reference to what has gone before, particularly in regard to any legitimate expectation that may be held (*Isleworth Crown Court, ex parte Irwin, The Times*, 5 December 1991, DC).

Range of Disposals

The Supreme Court Act 1981, s. 48:

48(1)   The Crown Court may, in the course of hearing any appeal, correct any error or mistake in the order or judgment incorporating the decision which is the subject of the appeal.

(2)   On the termination of the hearing of an appeal the Crown Court—

(a)   may confirm, reverse or vary any part of the decision appealed against, including a determination not to impose a separate penalty in respect of an offence; or

(b)   may remit the matter with its opinion thereon to the authority whose decision is appealed against; or

(c)   may make such order in the matter as the court thinks just, and by such order exercise any power which the said authority might have exercised.

(3)   Subsection (2) has effect subject to any enactment relating to any such appeal which expressly limits or restricts the powers of the court on the appeal.

(4)   Subject to section 11(6) of the Criminal Appeal Act 1995, if the appeal is against a conviction or a sentence, the preceding provisions of this section shall be construed as including power to award any punishment, whether more or less severe than that awarded by the magistrates' court whose decision is appealed against, if that is a punishment which that magistrates' court might have awarded.

(5)   This section applies whether or not the appeal is against the whole of the decision.

(6)   In this section 'sentence' includes any order made by the court when dealing with an offender, including—

(a)   a hospital order under Part III of the Mental Health Act 1983, with or without a restriction order, and an interim hospital order under that Act; and

(b)   a recommendation for deportation made when dealing with an offender.

(7)   The fact that an appeal is pending against an interim hospital order under the said Act of 1983 shall not affect the power of the magistrates' court that made it to renew or terminate the order or to deal with the appellant on its termination; and where the Crown Court quashes such an order but does not pass any sentence or make any other order in its place the Court may direct the appellant to be kept in custody or released on bail pending his being dealt with by that magistrates' court.

(8)   Where the Crown Court makes an interim hospital order by virtue of subsection (2)—

(a)   the power of renewing or terminating the order and of dealing with the appellant on its termination shall be exercisable by the magistrates' court whose decision is appealed against and not by the Crown Court; and

(b)   that magistrates' court shall be treated for the purposes of section 38(7) of the said Act of 1983 (absconding offenders) as the court that made the order.

The effect of section 48 is wide-ranging. In the event for example that an appellant appeals against a conviction in respect of only one offence, having been convicted on the same occasion of two or more, the court can still vary, if it wishes, the sentence not appealed against (*Dutta* v *Westcott* (1987) 84 Cr App R 103, DC).

In deciding what sentence might have been awarded, reference must be made to the date on which the magistrates passed sentence. In *Portsmouth Crown Court, ex parte Ballard, The Times*, 27 June 1989 DC, the court passed on appeal a sentence consecutive to one imposed after the magistrates' original sentence. Accordingly that sentence would not have been available to the lower court at the time.

The usual costs orders are available to the court.

FURTHER APPEALS

There is no appeal available to the Court of Appeal. The remaining remedies for an appellant who is still aggrieved are case stated, judicial review, Royal Pardon and references made by the Criminal Cases Review Commission.

6 Appeals in Respect of Bail

INTRODUCTION

The liberty of the subject should be the fundamental concern of any criminal court. The quality of decision making, in respect of bail, varies considerably between courts, with some justices being thought of as employees of the prosecuting authorities. In recent years the Government itself has become concerned with decision making in respect of bail, and has given the prosecution powers, in certain cases, to appeal the grant of bail by justices. From a client care point of view, the ability to inform the detained client, quickly and knowledgably, of appeal remedies is one of the basic prerequisites of being a competent criminal advocate.

It would be trite to remind the practitioner of the number of bail applications that can be made before the justices, and therefore this chapter is devoted to remedies before the Crown Court and the High Court, available to both defence and prosecution.

OPTION OF JUDICIAL REVIEW

The general rule that where there is another available remedy, judicial review will not be allowed, applies equally to bail decisions. A defendant must first exhaust all remedies before even contemplating judicial review proceedings (*Re Herbage*, *The Times*, 25 October 1985, DC; *Croydon Crown Court, ex parte Cox* [1997] 1 Cr App R 20, DC).

CROWN COURT JURISDICTION

The Crown Court's jurisdiction in respect of bail derives from s. 81, Supreme Court Act 1981, which provides:

81(1)   The Crown Court may, subject to section 25 of the Criminal Justice and Public Order Act 1994, grant bail to any person—

(a)   who has been committed in custody for appearance before the Crown Court or in relation to whose case a notice of transfer has been given under a relevant transfer provision; or

(b)   who is in custody pursuant to a sentence imposed by a magistrates' court, and who has appealed to the Crown Court against his conviction or sentence; or

(c)   who is in the custody of the Crown Court pending the disposal of his case by that court; or

(d)   who, after the decision of his case by the Crown Court, has applied to that court for the statement of a case for the High Court on that decision; or

(e)   who has applied to the High Court for an order of certiorari to remove proceedings in the Crown Court in his case into the High Court, or has applied to the High Court for leave to make such an application; or

(f)   [not reproduced here]; or

(g)   who has been remanded in custody by a magistrates' court on adjourning a case under—

(i)   section 5 (adjournment of inquiry into offence);

(ii)   section 10 (adjournment of trial);

(iii)   section 18 (initial procedure on information against adult for offences triable either way); or

(iv)   section 30 (remand for medical examination),

of the Magistrates' Courts Act 1980;

and the time during which a person is released on bail under any provision of this subsection shall not count as part of any term of imprisonment or detention under his sentence.

(1A)–(1G) [Dealt with later in this work.]

(1H)   Where the Crown Court grants a person bail under subsection (1)(g) it may direct him to appear at a time and place which the magistrates' court could have directed and the recognizance of any surety shall be conditioned accordingly.

(1J)   The Crown Court may only grant bail to a person under subsection (1)(g) if the magistrates' court which remanded him in custody has certified under section 5(6A) of the Bail Act 1976 that it heard full argument on his application for bail before it refused the application.

(2)   [Not reproduced here.]

(3)   Any reference in any enactment to a recognizance shall include, unless the context otherwise requires, a reference to any other description of security given instead of a recognizance, whether in pursuance of subsection (2)(a) or otherwise.

(4)   The Crown Court, on issuing a warrant for the arrest of any person, may endorse the warrant for bail, and in any such case—

(a)   the person arrested under the warrant shall, unless the Crown Court otherwise directs, be taken to a police station; and

(b)   the officer in charge of the station shall release him from custody if he, and any sureties required by the endorsement and approved by the officer, enter into recognizances of such amount as may be fixed by the endorsement:

Provided that in the case of criminal proceedings (within the meaning of the Bail Act 1976) the person arrested shall not be required to enter into a recognizance.

(5) A person in custody in pursuance of a warrant issued by the Crown Court with a view to his appearance before that court shall be brought forthwith before either the Crown Court or a magistrates' court.

(6) A magistrates' court shall have jurisdiction, and a justice of the peace may act, under or in pursuance of rules under subsection (2) whether or not the offence was committed, or the arrest was made, within the court's area, or the area for which he was appointed.

(7) In subsection (1) above 'relevant transfer provision' means—
(a) section 4 of the Criminal Justice Act 1987, or
(b) section 53 of the Criminal Justice Act 1991.

It can be seen that the section covers all instances where bail has been refused by the magistrates' court, including situations where bail is sought pending appeal. In addition this is the route to be followed when bail is sought pending the determination of a judicial review or case stated.

PROCEDURE — DEFENCE APPLICATIONS

The Crown Court Rules, rr. 11A and 19–21, detail the procedures to be followed and are reproduced at the end of this chapter.

The following points apply:

● Save where the Official Solicitor is assigned, 24 hours' notice of intention to make a Crown Court bail application must be given to the prosecutor who, in the case of the Crown Prosecution Service, is the prosecutor assigned to the case.

● It is now usual practice to contact the Crown Court listing office for a convenient date in advance. This allows all parties to make sufficient arrangements in advance of the hearing, and generally expedites the process.

● A copy of the notice of appeal (a precedent is set out at the end of this chapter) must be given to the appropriate officer of the Crown Court. The rules do not specify when it should be served, but again it is good practice to serve it as soon as practicable, and there seems to be no good reason why it should not be served at the same date as the one served on the prosecution.

● A person who has not been able to instruct a solicitor to act on their behalf, may, when giving notice of an application to apply for bail, ask that the Official Solicitor be assigned to act on their behalf. If the Crown Court thinks fit, the Official Solicitor will be so assigned. In such a situation the Crown Court may dispense with the usual notice requirements and proceed to hear the application in a summary manner.

● An applicant is not entitled without leave to be present during the application, save where the application is one by the prosecutor or a constable under s. 3(8), Bail Act 1976 (variation of conditional bail). It is rare for a Crown Court to grant such leave.

● The application must be supported by a certificate of full argument (see s. 5, Bail Act 1976).

● It is the duty of the applicant to inform the Crown Court of any earlier applications for bail, in the same proceedings, to the Crown Court or the High Court.

● The prosecutor, upon receiving the notice of appeal, should notify the appropriate officer of the Crown Court and the applicant that (a) he wishes to be represented at the hearing or (b) that he does not oppose the application.

● Applications should be made to the court to which the case will be or would have been committed for trial. In the event of an application in a purely summary case it should be made to the Crown Court centre which normally receives class 4 work. The hearing will be listed as a chambers matter unless a judge has directed otherwise (*Practice Direction (Crown Court: Applications For Bail)* (1983) 77 Cr App R 69). Accordingly all solicitors have rights of audience in relation to the conduct of the application for bail.

● If the applicant is legally aided in the magistrates' court (either under an ordinary order or under an order limited to a bail application) the legal aid order covers applications under this procedure. If the applicant is not legally aided neither the Crown Court nor the magistrates' court has power to grant a legal aid order for the purpose of applications for bail to the Crown Court alone (*Practice Direction* above).

● Legal aid for this purpose is limited to representation by a solicitor unless the legal aid order granted by the magistrates' court specifically includes representation by counsel (*Practice Direction* above).

Excluded Applications

If the defendant is granted conditional bail, and wishes to apply to vary, application can be made to the magistrates' court or the High Court. The Crown Court has no jurisdiction to deal with variations at the behest of the defendant, except where that court originally granted bail, for example after an appeal from the magistrates' court.

Format of the Hearing

The hearings tend to be informal and if held in the judge's room, as opposed to a court sitting in camera, the parties are seated with both outlining their case.

The prosecution can choose to tender written objections and not to be represented. Such representations must be served on both the appropriate officer of the Crown Court and the applicant.

The prosecution are allowed a right of reply to correct misstatements of fact (*Isleworth Crown Court and D, ex parte Commissioners of Customs and Excise* [1991] COD 1, DC).

The judge announces the decision at the immediate conclusion of the hearing, and the Crown Court will notify the prison detaining the defendant in order to secure an immediate release (subject to any conditions having been met).

PROCEDURE — PROSECUTION APPLICATIONS

In certain instances the prosecution have the right to appeal the grant of bail by justices (Bail (Amendment) Act 1993, reproduced at the end of the chapter with the relevant Magistrates' Court rules). This has the effect of keeping the defendant in custody, to be brought before the Crown Court, for the issue to be determined.

Definition of 'Prosecutor'

Those prosecutors who act under the direction of the following authorities have powers under the Act, in respect of bail appeals (Bail (Amendment) Act 1993 (Prescription of Prosecuting Authorities) Order 1994, SI 1994/1438):

- Crown prosecutors (by virtue of s. 1(2)(a) of the Act);
- Serious Fraud Office and any person designated under s. 1(7), Criminal Justice Act 1987;
- Department of Trade and Industry;
- Customs and Excise;
- Department of Social Security;
- Post Office;
- Commissioners of the Inland Revenue.

Use of the Power

The Crown Prosecution Service has indicated that the appeal of bail will happen in very few instances. The use of the power indicates directly to the justices that their decision is thought to be wrong: accordingly, the wholesale use of the power has the potential to lead to ill-feeling between prosecutors and justices.

The Crown Prosecution Service has issued the following guidance:

- The power of appeal against a grant of bail must be used judiciously and responsibly and the CPS expects the number of appeals to be small. It is not to be used merely because the Crown prosecutor disagrees with the decision of the magistrates.
- It should only be used in cases of grave concern. Prosecutors should apply an overarching test of whether there is a serious risk of harm to any member of the public or other significant public interest grounds. In deciding whether this test is satisfied, the nature and seriousness of the offence may be relevant if they illustrate the risk created by granting bail.
- The guidance is not exhaustive, but sets out some examples. An appeal may be made in offences which put lives at risk and cases of personal violence, particularly if weapons are alleged to have been used. The right of appeal is not to be used automatically in cases in which the magistrates must give reasons for granting bail.
- The following are factors which may be relevant when deciding whether an appeal is justified:

(a)   the risk to victims, e.g. if the defendant's record discloses previous
convictions of a similar kind, against the same victim or a similar type of victim;

(b)   a strong indication that the defendant may abscond, particularly if he or she
has no right to remain in Britain or has substantial assets or interests abroad;

(c)   lack of established identity or of any community ties, for example in cases of
terrorism, offences involving national security or drug trafficking on a large scale.

● The CPS ensures that, wherever possible, approval is sought in advance of the
hearing from a Crown prosecutor of at least four years' experience. At court the
Crown prosecutor takes into account any information given to the magistrates by the
defendant or defence lawyer, as well as information provided by the Probation
Service. Once the written notice of appeal has been served, the file is further
reviewed before the final decision to proceed with the appeal is taken.

Criteria

The magistrates must have granted bail to a person who is charged with or convicted of:

● an offence punishable by a term of imprisonment of five years or more. In
relation to a child or young person, this means in reference to an offence which would
be so punishable in the case of an adult (s. 1(10)(a) of the Act); or
● an offence of taking a vehicle without authority or aggravated vehicle taking.
and:
● that such an appeal can only be made if the prosecution made representations,
before bail was granted, that bail should not be granted.

Making the Appeal

There are two stages, the oral notice of appeal and the written notice.

● *Oral notice*   Section 1(4) provides that oral notice must be given to the court
and defendant, at the conclusion of the proceedings in which bail was granted and
before the release of the person concerned. In *Isleworth Crown Court, ex parte
Clarke*, QBD, No. CO/2433/97, oral notice was held to have been given to the court,
when it was given to the court clerk about five minutes after the court rose.
   Rule 93A, Magistrates' Courts Rules 1981 (see end of chapter), prescribes the
court procedures to be followed, which include (1) the clerk announcing in court the
time that oral notice was given, and (2) a record of the appeal and time made being
recorded in the court register. Once oral notice has been given the defendant must be
remanded into custody.
● *Written notice*   Written notice must be served upon the court and defendant
within two hours. Upon receipt of written notice the court will again remand the
defendant into custody until the determination of the appeal, or other disposal (for
example, abandonment of the appeal).

If the prosecutor fails to serve written notice within two hours the court must direct the immediate release of the defendant, subject to the conditions, if any, of the original bail decision. A form of notice of appeal can be found at the end of the chapter.

The Appeal Hearing

The hearing at the Crown Court follows the same format as a normal bail hearing, with the prosecution outlining their objections.

HIGH COURT BAIL APPLICATIONS

The High Court has concurrent jurisdiction in respect of bail decisions. The usual course is to proceed in turn from the magistrates' court to the Crown Court and finally to the High Court. Where an appellant is aggrieved at the conditions imposed by justices, the only avenue of appeal is to the High Court (Criminal Justice Act 1967, s. 22(1)).

Legal Aid

The Legal Aid Board gives the following guidance in relation to applications for civil legal aid, to cover High Court bail applications:

An application for legal aid to cover an application for bail to the High Court is likely to be refused if it appears more appropriate to rely on the Official Solicitor procedure under RSC Ord. 79, i.e. where the application is simple without the need for a significant degree of preparation or legal argument. A civil legal aid application for bail to the judge in chambers should include information on the following:

(a) whether the defendant is in the custody of the magistrates' court or the Crown Court;

(b) the length of time the defendant would otherwise be likely to remain in custody pending trial;

(c) whether the defendant has already applied for bail to the magistrates' court and/or Crown Court (bail is often granted on a subsequent appearance when difficulties relating to sureties have been sorted out);

(d) whether the defendant has been represented on previous applications for bail;

(e) why bail was refused and whether it is suggested that the reasons given by the court for refusing bail were unreasonable or the grounds for refusing bail have altered;

(f) any special social or other reasons for making an application for bail in the particular case.

Since the chances of obtaining civil legal aid are slim in the extreme, practitioners may feel able to cover initial costs, including drafting the order and affidavit (and disbursement for swearing it), on a Claim 14. The subsequent appearance would of course be unremunerated, which is less of a problem for practitioners near to a Crown Court centre with a resident High Court judge.

Making the Application

Order 79, r. 9 sets out the procedure, and is reproduced in full below. The main points are:

- the application is made by summons, supported by affidavit, and certificate of full argument/record of bail decision;
- summons must be served on the prosecutor at least 24 hours before the hearing;
- application is heard in chambers. Informal procedure;
- if the application is refused, r. 9(12) prevents a further application.

CONCLUSION

It is important to utilise fully the many bail applications and appeals available. Most practitioners will testify to the reasonableness of High Court judges when considering bail — the one drawback being the almost total lack of legal aid available for the purpose. A well structured bail application, with sensible conditions being proposed, can often tip the balance. In almost all cases, solicitors with conduct of the case will be in a position to argue the merits of the case more fully than counsel who only picked up the brief minutes before.

NOTICE OF APPLICATION RELATING TO BAIL TO
BE MADE TO THE CROWN COURT

AT MANCHESTER CROWN COURT

NAME OF MAGISTRATES' COURT: MANCHESTER MAGISTRATES' COURT

CROWN SQUARE, MANCHESTER, M1

TAKE NOTICE that an Application relating to bail will be made to the Crown Court

at: MANCHESTER CROWN COURT
on: 7 JULY 1998 at 9.45 am   **[arrange time with listing office]**

on behalf of the Defendant/Appellant/Respondent

1.   DEFENDANT/APPELLANT

SURNAME: KEOGH   **DOB**: 03/07/70
FORENAMES: ANDREW WILLIAM

ADDRESS: 1 THE TUDORS, MANCHESTER M1 2AB

2.   SOLICITORS

FREEEM QUICK & CO., 12 THE PARADE, MANCHESTER M1 2XY

3.   IF IN CUSTODY STATE DETAILS

PLACE OF DETENTION: HMP STRANGEWAYS, MANCHESTER
PRISON NUMBER: XYZ123ERS

TIME IN CUSTODY: SINCE 1 JUNE 1998

DATE OF LAST REMAND: 15 JUNE 1998

4.   STAGE OF PROCEEDINGS

AWAITING PREPARATION OF COMMITTAL PAPERS

5.   OFFENCE ALLEGED

POSSESSION OF CLASS A DRUGS (HEROIN) 100 KILOGRAMMMES

6. IF CASE PENDING BEFORE MAGISTRATES, GIVE DETAILS

NEXT HEARING MANCHESTER MAGISTRATES' COURT, 9 JULY 1998, 10AM

7. DETAILS OF PREVIOUS BAIL APPLICATIONS

BAIL REFUSED BY MAGISTRATES ON 15 JUNE 1998, FOLLOWING THE SECOND FULL APPLICATION FOR BAIL

8. NATURE AND GROUNDS OF APPLICATION

It is accepted that the defendant faces a grave allegation, carrying, upon conviction, a lengthy custodial sentence.

The defendant was arrested on the 31st May 1998, at his home address, following the execution of a search warrant at those premises.

During the search, the drugs were found in an unlocked garden shed to the side of the property. The defendant, present at the time of the search (at 5.25am), had returned 3 hours earlier from a family holiday in Turkey. Also present were his wife and two children (aged 3 and 4 years). At this stage there appears to be no other evidence, and there is no allegation that they were imported when he returned from holiday.

The defence will call evidence to show that on the 29th May an intruder was seen on the defendant's premises, and the police were called. A cursory search revealed nothing had been disturbed or taken.

The defendant maintains that he knows nothing of the drugs. The defendant is a man of 27 years of age, of previous good character, and a partner with a local firm of accountants.

There is a presumption in favour of bail. The defendant has a stable home address, significant community ties (14 family members living within 3 miles of his home), and his children in local nurseries.

Bail was denied on the grounds that there were substantial grounds for believing that if admitted to bail, he would fail to surrender.

The defendant can offer to sign on daily at his local police station and surrender his passport. His fellow partners are able to stand surety of £100,000.

Accordingly, I respectfully ask that this Court admit the defendant to bail.

Signed

Solicitor for Defendant.

CROWN COURT RULES, rr. 11A, 19–21

11A(1) This rule shall apply where the prosecution appeals under section 1 of the Bail (Amendment) Act 1993 against a decision of a magistrates' court granting bail and in this rule, 'the 1993 Act' means that Act and 'the person concerned' has the same meaning as in that Act.

(2) The written notice of appeal required by section 1(5) of the 1993 Act shall be in the form prescribed in Schedule 9 or a form to the like effect and shall be served on—

    (a) the clerk of the magistrates' court

    (b) the person concerned.

(3) The appropriate officer of the Crown Court shall enter the appeal and give notice of the time and place of the hearing to—

    (a) the prosecution

    (b) the person concerned or his legal representative

    (c) the clerk of the magistrates' court.

(4) The person concerned shall not be entitled to be present at the hearing of the appeal unless he is acting in person, or, in any other case of an exceptional nature, a judge of the Crown Court is of the opinion that the interests of justice require him to be present and gives him leave to be so.

(5) Where a person concerned has not been able to instruct a solicitor to represent him at the appeal, he may give notice to the Crown Court requesting that the Official Solicitor shall represent him at the appeal, and the court may, if it thinks fit, assign the Official Solicitor to act for the person concerned accordingly.

(6) At any time after the service of written notice of appeal under paragraph (2) above, the prosecution may abandon the appeal by giving notice in writing in the form prescribed in Schedule 10 or a form to the like effect.

(7) The notice of abandonment required by the preceding paragraph shall be served on—

    (a) the person concerned or his legal representative

    (b) the clerk of the magistrates' court

    (c) the appropriate officer of the Crown Court.

(8) Any record required by section 5 of the Bail Act 1976 (together with any note of reasons required by subsection (4) of that section to be included) shall be made by way of an entry in the file relating to the case in question and the record shall include the following particulars, namely—

    (a) the effect of the decision

    (b) a statement of any condition imposed in respect of bail, indicating whether it is to be complied with before or after release on bail

    (c) where bail is withheld, a statement of the relevant exception to the right to bail (as provided in Schedule 1 to the said Act of 1976) on which the decision is based.

(9) The appropriate officer of the Crown Court shall, as soon as practicable after the hearing of the appeal, give notice of the decision and of the matters required by the preceding paragraph to be recorded to—

(a)   the person concerned or his legal representative

(b)   the prosecution

(c)   the police

(d)   the clerk of the magistrates' court

(e)   the governor of the prison or person responsible for the establishment where the person concerned is being held.

(10)   Where the judge hearing the appeal grants bail to the person concerned, the provisions of rule 20 shall apply as if that person had applied to the Crown Court for bail.

(11)   In addition to the methods of service permitted by rule 28, the notices required by paragraphs (3), (5), (7) and (9) of this rule may be sent by way of facsimile transmission and the notice required by paragraph (3) may be given by telephone.

. . .

19(1)   This Rule applies where an application to the Crown Court relating to bail is made otherwise than during the hearing of proceedings in the Crown Court.

(2)   Subject to paragraph (7), notice in writing of intention to make such an application to the Crown Court shall, at least 24 hours before it is made, be given to the prosecutor and if the prosecution is being carried on by the Crown Prosecution Service, to the appropriate Crown Prosecutor or, if the application is to be made by the prosecutor or a constable under section 3(8) of the Bail Act 1976, to the person to whom bail was granted.

(3)   On receiving notice under paragraph (2), the prosecutor or appropriate Crown Prosecutor or, as the case may be, the person to whom bail was granted shall—

(a)   notify the appropriate officer of the Crown Court and the applicant that he wishes to be represented at the hearing of the application; or

(b)   notify the appropriate officer and the applicant that he does not oppose the application; or

(c)   give to the appropriate officer, for the consideration of the Crown Court, a written statement of his reasons for opposing the application, at the same time sending a copy of the statement to the applicant.

(4)   A notice under paragraph (2) shall be in the form prescribed in Schedule 4 or a form to the like effect, and the applicant shall give a copy of the notice to the appropriate officer of the Crown Court.

(5)   Except in the case of an application made by the prosecutor or a constable under section 3(8) of the Bail Act 1976, the applicant shall not be entitled to be present on the hearing of his application unless the Crown Court gives him leave to be present.

(6)   Where a person who is in custody or has been released on bail desires to make an application relating to bail and has not been able to instruct a solicitor to apply on his behalf under the preceding paragraphs of this Rule, he may give notice in writing to the Crown Court of his desire to make an application relating to bail, requesting that the Official Solicitor shall act for him in the application, and the Court may, if it thinks fit, assign the Official Solicitor to act for the applicant accordingly.

(7)   Where the Official Solicitor has been so assigned the Crown Court may, if it thinks fit, dispense with the requirements of paragraph (2) and deal with the application in a summary manner.

(8)   Any record required by section 5 of the Bail Act 1976 (together with any note of reasons required by subsection (4) of that section to be included) shall be made by way of an entry in the file relating to the case in question and the record shall include the following particulars, namely—

(a)   the effect of the decision

(b)   a statement of any condition imposed in respect of bail, indicating whether it is to be complied with before or after release on bail

(c)   where conditions of bail are varied, a statement of the conditions as varied

(d)   where bail is withheld, a statement of the relevant exception to the right to bail (as provided in Schedule 1 to the said Act of 1976) on which the decision is based.

20(1)   Every person who makes an application to the Crown Court relating to bail shall inform the Court of any earlier application to the High Court or the Crown Court relating to bail in the course of the same proceedings.

(2)   Where the Crown Court grants bail in criminal proceedings, the recognizance of any surety required as a condition of bail may be entered into before an officer of the Crown Court or, where the person who has been granted bail is in a prison or other place of detention, before the governor or keeper of the prison or place as well as before the persons specified in section 8(4) of the Bail Act 1976.

(3)   Where the Crown Court under section 3(5) or (6) of the Bail Act 1976 imposes a requirement to be complied with before a person's release on bail, the Court may give directions as to the manner in which and the person or persons before whom the requirement may be complied with.

. . .

(5)   A person who, in pursuance of an order made by the Crown Court for the grant of bail in criminal proceedings, proposes to enter into a recognizance or give security must, unless the Crown Court otherwise directs, give notice to the prosecutor at least 24 hours before he enters into the recognizance or gives security as aforesaid.

(6)   Where, in pursuance of an order of the Crown Court, a recognizance is entered into or any requirement imposed under section 3(5) or (6) is complied with (being a requirement to be complied with before a person's release on bail) before any person, it shall be his duty to cause the recognizance or, as the case may be, a statement of the requirement to be transmitted forthwith to the appropriate officer of the Crown Court; and a copy of the recognizance or statement shall at the same time be sent to the governor or keeper of the prison or other place of detention in which the person named in the order is detained, unless the recognizance was entered into or the requirement was complied with before such governor or keeper.

(7)   Where, in pursuance of section 3(5) of the Bail Act 1976, security has been given in respect of a person granted bail with a duty to surrender to the custody of the Crown Court and either—

(a)   that person surrenders to the custody of the Court; or

(b)   that person having failed to surrender to the custody of the Court, the Court decides not to order the forfeiture of the security,

the appropriate officer of the Court shall as soon as practicable give notice of the surrender to custody or, as the case may be, of the decision not to forfeit the security to the person before whom the security was given.

(8)   In this Rule 'bail in criminal proceedings' has the same meaning as in the Bail Act 1976.

. . .

21(1)   Where a recognizance has been entered into in respect of a person granted bail to appear before the Crown Court and it appears to the Court that a default has been made in performing the conditions of the recognizance, the Court may order the recognizance to be estreated.

(2)   Where the Crown Court is to consider making an order under paragraph (1) for a recognizance to be estreated, the appropriate officer of the Court shall give notice to that effect to the person by whom the recognizance was entered into indicating the time and place at which the matter will be considered; and no such order shall be made before the expiry of seven days after the notice required by this paragraph has been given.

BAIL AMENDMENT ACT 1993

1(1)   Where a magistrates' court grants bail to a person who is charged with or convicted of—

(a)   an offence punishable by a term of imprisonment of five years or more, or

(b)   an offence under section 12 (taking a conveyance without authority) or 12A (aggravated vehicle taking) of the Theft Act 1968,

the prosecution may appeal to a judge of the Crown Court against the granting of bail.

(2)   Subsection (1) above applies only where the prosecution is conducted—

(a)   by or on behalf of the Director of Public Prosecutions; or

(b)   by a person who falls within such class or description of person as may be prescribed for the purposes of this section by order made by the Secretary of State.

(3)   Such an appeal may be made only if—

(a)   the prosecution made representations that bail should not be granted; and

(b)   the representations were made before it was granted.

(4)   In the event of the prosecution wishing to exercise the right of appeal set out in subsection (1) above, oral notice of appeal shall be given to the magistrates' court at the conclusion of the proceedings in which such bail has been granted and before the release from custody of the person concerned.

(5)   Written notice of appeal shall thereafter be served on the magistrates' court and the person concerned within two hours of the conclusion of such proceedings.

(6)   Upon receipt from the prosecution of oral notice of appeal from its decision to grant bail the magistrates' court shall remand in custody the person concerned, until the appeal is determined or otherwise disposed of.

(7)   Where the prosecution fails, within the period of two hours mentioned in subsection (5) above, to serve one or both of the notices required by that subsection, the appeal shall be deemed to have been disposed of.

(8)   The hearing of an appeal under subsection (1) above against a decision of the magistrates' court to grant bail shall be commenced within forty-eight hours, excluding weekends and any public holiday (that is to say, Christmas Day, Good Friday or a bank holiday), from the date on which oral notice of appeal is given.

(9)   At the hearing of any appeal by the prosecution under this section, such appeal shall be by way of re-hearing, and the judge hearing any such appeal may remand the person concerned in custody or may grant bail subject to such conditions (if any) as he thinks fit.

(10)   In relation to a child or young person (within the meaning of the Children and Young Persons Act 1969)—

(a)   the reference in subsection (1) above to an offence punishable by a term of imprisonment is to be read as a reference to an offence which would be so punishable in the case of an adult; and

(b)   the reference in subsection (6) above to remand in custody is to be read subject to the provisions of section 23 of the Act of 1969 (remands to local authority accommodation).

(11)   The power to make an order under subsection (2) above shall be exercisable by statutory instrument and any instrument shall be subject to annulment in pursuance of a resolution of either House of Parliament.

MAGISTRATES' COURT RULES
Magistrates' Courts Rules 1981, r. 93A
Procedure where prosecution appeals against a decision to grant bail

93A(1)   Where the prosecution wishes to exercise the right of appeal, under section 1 of the Bail (Amendment) Act 1993 (hereafter in this rule referred to as 'the 1993 Act'), to a judge of the Crown Court against a decision to grant bail, the oral notice of appeal must be given to the clerk of the magistrates' court and to the person concerned, at the conclusion of the proceedings in which such bail was granted and before the release of the person concerned.

(2)   When oral notice of appeal is given, the clerk of the magistrates' court shall announce in open court the time at which such notice was given.

(3)   A record of the prosecution's decision to appeal and the time the oral notice of appeal was given shall be made in the register and shall contain the particulars set out in the appropriate form prescribed for the purpose.

(4)   Where an oral notice of appeal has been given the court shall remand the person concerned in custody by a warrant of commitment in the appropriate form prescribed for the purpose.

(5)   On receipt of the written notice of appeal required by section 1(5) of the 1993 Act, the court shall remand the person concerned in custody by a warrant of commitment in the appropriate form prescribed for the purpose, until the appeal is determined or otherwise disposed of.

(6)   A record of the receipt of the written notice of appeal shall be made in the same manner as that of the oral notice of appeal under paragraph (3) above.

(7)   If, having given oral notice of appeal, the prosecution fails to serve a written notice of appeal within the two hour period referred to in section 1(5) of the 1993 Act the clerk of the magistrates' court shall, as soon as practicable, by way of written notice to the persons in whose custody the person concerned is, direct the release of the person concerned on bail as granted by the magistrates' court and subject to any conditions which it imposed.

(8)   If the prosecution serves notice of abandonment of appeal on the clerk of the magistrates' court, the clerk shall, forthwith, by way of written notice to the Governor of the prison where the person concerned is being held, or the person responsible for any other establishment where such a person is being held, direct his release on bail as granted by the magistrates' court and subject to any conditions which it imposed.

(9)   The clerk of the magistrates' court shall record the prosecution's failure to serve a written notice of appeal, or its service of a notice of abandonment in the appropriate form prescribed for the purpose.

(10)   Where a written notice of appeal has been served on the clerk of the magistrates' court, he shall provide as soon as practicable to the appropriate officer of the Crown Court a copy of that written notice, together with—

(a)   the notes of argument made by the clerk of the court under rule 90A of these Rules, and

(b)   a note of the date, or dates, when the person concerned is next due to appear in the magistrates' court, whether he is released on bail or remanded in custody by the Crown Court.

(11)   References in this rule to 'the person concerned' are references to such a person within the meaning of section 1 of the 1993 Act.

BAIL (AMENDMENT) ACT 1993 — NOTICE OF APPEAL

Notice of appeal by the Prosecution under section 1 of the Bail (Amendment) Act 1993, against the granting of bail.

- Written notice of appeal must be served within 2 hours of the conclusion of the proceedings in which oral notice of appeal was given (s. 1(5)).
- Copies of this notice must be served on the Magistrates' Court and the person concerned (s. 1(5)).
- The hearing of the appeal must be commenced within 48 hours from the date on which oral notice of appeal was given. This excludes weekends, Christmas Day, Good Friday and Bank Holidays.

Court:

Defendant:

Address:

Charge(s):

Date of grant of bail:
Date and time of oral notice:

TAKE NOTICE THAT, oral notice of appeal against the granting of bail to the aforementioned having been given at the time, date and place set out above, I, a person conducting a prosecution on behalf of the Director of Public Prosecutions [or other authorised body], hereby give written notice of appeal in accordance with section 1(5) of the 1993 Act.

PAGE 1 OF 2

The grounds of this appeal are:

_____

Name of Prosecutor:

Address:

Date and time of service of notice on clerk of the court:

Date and time of service of notice on defendant:

_____

RSC 1965 (SI 1965/1776), Ord. 79, r. 9

9(1)   Subject to the provisions of this rule, every application to the High Court in respect of bail in any criminal proceedings—

(a)   where the defendant is in custody, must be made by summons before a judge in chambers to show cause why the defendant should not be granted bail;

(b)   where the defendant has been admitted to bail, must be made by summons before a judge in chambers to show cause why the variation in the arrangements for bail proposed by the applicant should not be made.

(2)   Subject to paragraph (5), the summons (in Form No. 97 or 97A in Appendix A) must, at least 24 hours before the day named therein for the hearing be served—

(a)   where the application was made by the defendant, on the prosecutor and on the Director of Public Prosecutions, if the prosecution is being carried on by him;

(b)   where the application was made by the prosecutor or a constable under section 3(8) of the Bail Act 1976, on the defendant;

and Order 32, rule 5 shall apply in relation to the summons.

(3)   Subject to paragraph (5), every application must be supported by affidavit.

(4)   Where a defendant in custody who desires to apply for bail is unable through lack of means to instruct a solicitor, he may give notice in writing to the judge in chambers stating his desire to apply for bail and requesting that the official solicitor shall act for him in the application, and the judge may, if he thinks fit, assign the official solicitor to act for the applicant accordingly.

(5)   Where the official solicitor has been so assigned the judge may, if he thinks fit, dispense with the requirements of paragraphs (1) to (3) and deal with the application in a summary manner.

(6)   Where the judge in chambers by whom an application for bail in criminal proceedings is heard grants the defendant bail, the order must be in Form No. 98 in Appendix A and a copy of the order shall be transmitted forthwith—

(a)   where the defendant has been committed to the Crown Court for trial or to be sentenced or otherwise dealt with, to the appropriate officer of the Crown Court;

(b)   in any other case, to the clerk of the court which committed the defendant.

(6A)   The recognizance of any surety required as a condition of bail granted as aforesaid may, where the defendant is in a prison or other place of detention, be entered into before the governor or keeper of the prison or place as well as before the persons specified in section 8(4) of the Bail Act 1976.

(6B)   Where under section 3(5) or (6) of the Bail Act 1976 a judge in chambers imposes a requirement to be complied with before a person's release on bail, the judge may give directions as to the manner in which and the person or persons before whom the requirement may be complied with.

(7)   A person who in pursuance of an order for the grant of bail made by a judge under this rule proposes to enter into a recognizance or give security must, unless the judge otherwise directs, give notice (in Form No. 100 in Appendix A) to the prosecutor at least 24 hours before he enters into the recognizance or complies with the requirement as aforesaid.

(8)   Where in pursuance of such order as aforesaid a recognizance is entered into or requirement complied with before any person, it shall be the duty of that person to cause the recognizance or, as the case may be, a statement of the requirement complied with to be transmitted forthwith—

(a)   where the defendant has been committed to the Crown Court for trial or to be sentenced or otherwise dealt with, to the appropriate officer of the Crown Court;

(b)   in any other case, to the clerk of the court which committed the defendant; and a copy of such recognizance or statement shall at the same time be sent to the governor or keeper of the prison or other place of detention in which the defendant is detained, unless the recognizance was entered into or the requirement complied with before such governor or keeper.

(9)   [Revoked.]

(10)   An order by the judge in chambers varying the arrangements under which the defendant has been granted bail shall be in Form 98A in Appendix A and a copy of the order shall be transmitted forthwith—

(a)   where the defendant has been committed to the Crown Court for trial or to be sentenced or otherwise dealt with, to the appropriate officer of the Crown Court;

(b)   in any other case, to the clerk of the court which committed the defendant.

(11)   Where in pursuance of an order of a judge in chambers or of the Crown Court a person is released on bail in any criminal proceeding pending the determination of an appeal to the High Court or House of Lords or an application for an order of certiorari, then, upon the abandonment of the appeal or application, or upon the decision of the High Court or House of Lords being given, any justice (being a justice acting for the same petty sessions area as the magistrates' court by which that person was convicted or sentenced) may issue process for enforcing the decision in respect of which such appeal or application was brought or, as the case may be, the decision of the High Court or House of Lords.

(12)   If an applicant to the High Court in any criminal proceedings is refused bail by a judge in chambers, the applicant shall not be entitled to make a fresh application for bail to any other judge or to a Divisional Court.

(13)   The record required by section 5 of the Bail Act 1976 to be made by the High Court shall be made by including in the file relating to the case in question a copy of the relevant order of the Court and shall contain the particulars set out in Form No. 98 or 98A in Appendix A, whichever is appropriate, except that in the case of a decision to withhold bail the record shall be made by inserting a statement of the decision on the Court's copy of the relevant summons and including it in the file relating to the case in question.

Summons and Affidavit in support — High Court Bail Variation

IN THE HIGH COURT OF JUSTICE

QUEEN'S BENCH DIVISION

SITTING AT BIRMINGHAM CROWN COURT

Let all parties concerned attend the judge in chambers on the 8th Day of April 1998, at 9.45am, on the hearing of an application on behalf of Anthony John Wass that the terms on which Anthony Carl Wass was granted bail by the Justices sitting at Sutton Pidding Youth Court on the 1st April 1998, should be varied as follows:

Terms on which bail was granted:
    (1)   Reside at 17 Kreswood Drive, Walmlen, save between the inclusive dates of the 9th–12th April when he should reside at 50 Peville Road, Hastings in the County of Sussex.
    (2)   Observe a curfew between the hours of 9pm and 7am, and present himself to any Police Officer attending at his place of residence.
    (3)   Keep away from Sta's newsagents Pinworth.
    (4)   Not to enter Cottage Lane Pinworth.

Proposed Variation:
That the curfew condition should be amended to read as follows:

Observe a curfew between the hours of 9pm and 7am, and present himself to any police officer attending at his place of residence. Save that the curfew shall not apply when he is in the company of Kevin Michael Polbey (His Guardian) or Annika Wass (His Mother).

Dated the 2nd Day of April 1998.
This summons was taken out by Andrew Keogh, Solicitor for Anthony John Wass.

Appeals in Respect of Bail

1st Affidavit of Andrew Keogh

Solicitor for applicant

Filed this Day of   1998

IN THE HIGH COURT OF JUSTICE

QUEEN'S BENCH DIVISION

BETWEEN:

ANTHONY John WASS   Applicant

—and—

CROWN PROSECUTION SERVICE   Respondent

AFFIDAVIT IN SUPPORT OF BAIL VARIATION

I, Andrew Keogh, of Startwright and Clewis Solicitors, 5 Sagley Road East, Quinton, Birmingham, Solicitor for the above named Applicant MAKE OATH and say as follows:

1. I am a Solicitor of the Supreme Court, employed in the Criminal Litigation Department of Startwright and Clewis Solicitors. This firm acts for the Applicant, Anthony John Wass (16 years of age), in criminal proceedings currently before Sutton Pidding youth court.

2. The Applicant is currently charged with three criminal offences, namely: Robbery, Going Equipped to Steal and Being Drunk and Disorderly in a Public Place. The Robbery allegation is said to involve the Applicant assaulting another youth before riding off with his bicycle. In this matter there is a co-accused youth by the name of Freddie Smith. The allegation of Going Equipped to Steal involves the same co-defendant, it is alleged that the Applicant was in possession of a screwdriver, the co-accused in possession of a nine inch metal bar. The circumstances of the final matter respectfully speak for themselves. All matters are denied and will in due course proceed to trial.

3. On the 1st April 1998 the Applicant appeared before Sutton Pidding Youth Court, when the matter was adjourned until the 20th April 1998. The Justices allowed a bail variation in order to allow the Applicant to reside at an address in Hastings,

Sussex, between the dates of 9–12 April 1998. This was in order to facilitate a family holiday break. On the same occasion the Justices refused to vary bail to allow the curfew to be lifted whilst in the company of one or both of his parents.

4.   The applicant's mother is Mrs Annika Wass, his Guardian Mr Kevin Polbey. Mr Polbey states to myself that both parents feel restricted by the imposition of the curfew, as it prevents the family from being together as a cohesive family unit after 9pm. In order to ensure that their son is given the supervision expected of them, it is necessary for one or both of them to remain indoors with the Applicant after 9pm. Both parents view this as an unsatisfactory arrangement and one which causes themselves considerable inconvenience. Mr Polbey feels that the inclusion of Anthony in more 'adult like' activities, for example dining out and visiting friends, bowling, cinema, amongst other activities, would instil in the Applicant a more mature outlook on life, and remove him from the more undesirable elements within his peer group.

5.   Accordingly I ask that this Honourable Court give consideration to the making of this bail variation.

Sworn at   In the County of West Midlands
this   Day of   1998

Before me,   , A Commissioner for
oaths/Solicitor.

FORM OF SUMMONS — HIGH COURT BAIL APPLICATION

IN THE HIGH COURT OF JUSTICE

QUEEN'S BENCH DIVISION

SITTING AT BIRMINGHAM CROWN COURT [OR ROYAL COURTS OF JUSTICE].

Let all parties concerned attend the judge in chambers on the

Day of   199 , at [TIME], on the hearing of an application on behalf of [APPLICANT], to show cause why bail should not be granted, following a commitment by the [court] on the [DATE].

Dated the [DATE].
This summons was taken out by [NAME], Solicitor for
[APPLICANT]

7   Appeal Against the Refusal of Legal Aid

INTRODUCTION

For criminal practitioners in all but the most specialised private client firms, the grant of legal aid is the life blood of the practice. It has been a trend in recent years for magistrates' courts to become more demanding in the information they require (as a result of pressure from central Government) and more eager to refuse legal aid on the 'interests of justice' test. Figures indicate that there has been a steady rise in legal aid refusals, and the number of orders revoked is increasing month by month. Without doubt, a common reason for legal aid refusal is poorly completed application forms. It is vital that practitioners pay proper attention to the forms and ensure that they do not reflect a wasted opportunity to put a client's case for legal aid. The restrictive size of the boxes should not deter an applicant from providing fully argued reasons, on a separate sheet if necessary. It is interesting that practitioners are now almost resigned to the fact that most road traffic matters will not attract legal aid, despite it being one of the most complex and litigated areas of criminal law.

OBLIGATORY LEGAL AID

The following categories, subject to an applicant's financial eligibility, qualify for legal aid as of right:

- following committal for trial on a charge of murder;
- in respect of a person who faces a custodial sentence, and has not previously been sent to prison;
- in respect of a young offender facing detention in a young offender institution or the prospect of a secure training centre;
- when the court is considering a recommendation for deportation;

● when a person is kept in custody for the purposes of a report or other enquiries, in respect of sentencing;

● when a person, having been remanded in custody, is brought before a court and may again be remanded or committed in custody, and is not legally represented but wishes to be so. However, this grant of legal aid will only cover that part of the proceedings which relate to bail.

REFUSAL OF LEGAL AID

Legal aid can be refused on one or both of the following grounds:

● that it does not appear desirable in the interests of justice to grant legal aid; or
● it appears that the applicant's disposable income and capital are such that he is ineligible ('the means test').

Notification will be given in the prescribed form, and the applicant will be told of the methods of renewing the application.

At this point, there are two channels open to the applicant, one is an appeal to the Legal Aid Board Area Committee, the other is a renewal of the application to the court. One is without prejudice to the other, save that an appeal to the area committee must be made within 14 days of the initial refusal of legal aid so, if a further application is to be made to the court, then it must be done speedily. This will give sufficient time both for the court to reconsider it and, if that fails for a further appeal to be made, this time to the committee. It will be seen, however, that some refusals cannot be appealed to the area committee. Even so, speed is of no less importance since all practitioners wish to avoid the risk of doing unremunerated work.

RENEWAL TO THE COURT

The applicant can renew the application before the court or the 'proper officer' of the court (the clerk to the justices or a designated legal aid clerk).

If the application is renewed to the clerk (presumably with new representations), the application can be either granted or referred to the court. The clerk has no power to refuse a referred application. It might be thought to be tactically advantageous therefore always to seek reconsideration in the first instance by the clerk, but one should note that the clerk has power to refer the application to a court, and this court in practice consists of one justice of the peace, sitting in private, denying the applicant the opportunity to make oral representations.

If the application is renewed to the court, the court may grant the application, refuse it, or submit it to the clerk for further consideration. In such instances, the clerk can still only grant the application or once again place it before the court.

Reasons must be given for the refusal of legal aid, whether refused by the court or clerk.

Form of the Appeal

Whether the appeal is made to the court or to the clerk, the application must be considered afresh according to the criteria. However, when an appeal is referred by the clerk to the court, this is often done in private, the applicant not even being told of the reconsideration. It is not surprising that most applications referred in this way are refused.

Good practice dictates that in general the cross-referral of applications does not take place, theoretically the application could be sent between court and clerk indefinitely (although mandamus might lie to force the court to adjudicate). Most clerks who receive new arguments, but are not convinced that legal aid should be granted, simply notify the applicant and allow an opportunity to make oral representations before the court.

It is important for the court to remember that the consideration of an appeal is just that, and not a review of the clerk's decision. The court must exercise its own independent discretion (*Liverpool City Magistrates' Court, ex parte Banwell* [1998] COD 144, DC).

When submitting an appeal to the court or appropriate officer, the applicant must send a copy of the notice of refusal (Form 2).

APPEAL TO LEGAL AID BOARD AREA COMMITTEE

Regulation 15, Legal Aid in Criminal and Care Proceedings (General) Regulations 1989 (reproduced at the end of the chapter), allows applications for review to the area committee where:

the applicant is charged with an indictable offence, or an offence triable either way, or appears or is brought before a magistrates' court to be dealt with in respect of a sentence imposed or an order made in connection with such an offence.

The second part of the definition includes, for example, applications to remove disqualifications if the original offence was indictable or triable either way (*Crown Court at Liverpool, ex parte McCann* [1995] RTR 23).

Following the implementation of the Legal Aid in Criminal and Care Proceedings (General) (Amendment) Regulations 1998 (SI 1998/662), offences which are triable summarily by virtue of the value of the relevant property in the offence, for example criminal damage, do not come within the appeal procedures, even though they are (somewhat technically it might be thought) either way offences. This regulation came into force on 1 April 1998, and applies to all legal aid orders made after that date.

The following conditions also apply to applications for review under reg. 15:

● the application had been refused on the grounds that it was not in the interests of justice; and

● the original application was made no later than 21 days before the date fixed for trial (or enquiry), where such date had been fixed at the time the application was made.

Procedure

● Application must be made within 14 days of the notification of refusal of legal aid.
● The applicant must enclose Form 1 (the original legal aid application) which should be endorsed with the reasons for refusal, and Form 2, the notice of refusal.
● The application must be made on Form Crim 9 (although there is no legal basis for the legal aid board for insisting on this requirement). Such forms are available free from the Legal Aid Board. Following the implementation of CIS systems the new form (reproduced at the end of this chapter) will be APP 5.

The area committee may either grant or refuse legal aid.

FURTHER APPEALS

There is no further avenue of appeal, save by way of judicial review. The later chapter on judicial review gives a number of examples of such challenges.

Application for review of refusal of criminal legal aid

APP5

Please complete in block capitals

Your details

Title: _____ Initials: _____

Surname: _____

First name: _____

Surname at birth: _____
(if different)
Date of birth: _____/_____/_____

National insurance number: [| | | | | | | |]

Sex: ☐ Male ☐ Female

Marital status: ☐ Single ☐ Married ☐ Cohabiting

☐ Separated ☐ Divorced ☐ Widowed

Place of birth: _____ Job: _____
(town)
Current address: _____

Town: _____

County: _____ Postcode: _____

Acting solicitor's details

➤ *Please ask your solicitor to fill in this section.*

Legal aid supplier number: [| | | | | |] [| | | | |]

Name of firm: _____

Phone: _____

Name of acting solicitor: _____

➤ *The acting solicitor must have a valid practising certificate. The Board cannot pay for any work done during any period in which the acting solicitor does not have a practising certificate.*

Solicitor's reference: _____

Contact name for enquiries: _____

Page 1

Case details

What are the alleged offence(s)? _____

_____

_____

Date of main offence: _____/_____/_____

Are the offence(s) ☐ Triable either way   ☐ Indictable only

What is the date of the next hearing? ___/___/___ Name of Court: _____

What is the purpose of the next hearing? _____

How do you intend to plead? ☐ Not guilty   ☐ Guilty   ☐ Mixed plea

Reason(s) why you think legal aid should be granted

➤ *Complete the boxes in this section that apply to you and give brief details or reasons for each in the space provided.*

➤ *You may need the help of a solicitor to complete this section of the form.*

☐ It is likely that I will lose my liberty because:

I am subject to a: ☐ community service order ☐ deferment of sentence

☐ conditional discharge   ☐ supervision order   ☐ care order

☐ probation order   ☐ suspended or partly suspended prison sentence

Tell us the nature of the offence and when was the order made:

☐ It is likely that I will lose my livelihood because:

☐ It is likely that I will suffer serious damage to my reputation because:

☐ A substantial question of law is involved, namely:

Page 2

Reason(s) why you think legal aid should be granted

☐ I shall be unable to understand the court proceedings or state my own case because:

> ☐ My knowledge of English is inadequate

> ☐ I suffer from mental illness or mental or physical disability
> ➤ *Give details of the disability*

☐ Witnesses have to be traced or interviewed on my behalf;
➤ *Give details*

☐ The case involves expert cross examination of a prosecution witness because:

☐ It is in someone else's interests that I am represented because:

☐ Any other reason(s):

Enclosures
➤ *Only copies should be sent*

☐ Form 1 - Copy of the application for legal aid in criminal proceedings

☐ Form 2 - Copy of notification of refusal to grant legal aid issued by the Magistrates' Court

☐ Other ➤ *Give details*

Declaration to be signed by the applicant

As far as I know all the information I have given is true and I have not withheld any relevant information. I understand that if I knowingly give false information or withhold relevant information my criminal legal aid may be stopped or cancelled and criminal proceedings may be taken against me.

Signed: _____ Date: _____ / _____ / _____

Legal Aid in Criminal and Care Proceedings (General) Regulations 1989
(as amended)

13.   Where a magistrates' court or a justices' clerk has refused to make a legal aid order, the court or the justices' clerk shall determine—
(a)   the applicant's disposable income and disposable capital, and
(b)   the amount of any contribution which would have been payable and the manner in which it would be payable by the applicant or an appropriate contributor had a legal aid order been made,
and shall notify the applicant of the amounts so determined.

Renewal of application
14.—(1)   Without prejudice to the provisions of regulation 15, an applicant whose application under regulation 11 has been refused may renew his application either orally to the court or to the justices' clerk.
(2)   Where an application is renewed under paragraph (1), the applicant shall return the notice of refusal which he received under regulation 12 or any such notice received under regulation 17(4).
(3)   Where an application is renewed to the justices' clerk, he may either grant the application or refer it to the court or to a justice of the peace.
(4)   Where an application is renewed to the court, the court may grant or refuse the application or refer it to the justices' clerk.
(5)   The court or a justice of the peace to whom an application is referred under paragraph (3) or (6), may grant or refuse the application.
(6)   A justices' clerk to whom an application is referred under paragraph (4), may grant the application or refer it either back to the court or to a justice of the peace.
(7)   Except where the applicant is not required to furnish a statement of means under regulation 23(4), a legal aid order shall not be made where an application is renewed under paragraph (1) until the court, a justice of the peace or the justices' clerk has considered the applicant's statement of means.
(8)   Regulation 12 shall apply where an application is refused under this regulation with the modification that references to a magistrates' court shall be construed as including references to a justice of the peace.
(9)   In this regulation, 'a justice of the peace' means a justice of the peace who is entitled to sit as a member of the magistrates' court.

Application for review
15.—(1)   Where an application for a legal aid order has been refused after having been considered for the first time by a magistrates' court or a justices' clerk, the applicant may, subject to paragraph (2), apply for review to the appropriate area committee.
(2)   An application for review shall only lie to an area committee where—
(a)   the applicant is charged with an indictable offence or an offence which is triable either way or appears or is brought before a magistrates' court to be dealt with

in respect of a sentence imposed or an order made in connection with such an offence; and

    (b)   the application for a legal aid order has been refused on the ground specified in regulation 12(1)(a); and

    (c)   the application for a legal aid order was made no later than 21 days before the date fixed for the trial of an information or the inquiry into an offence as examining justices, where such a date had been fixed at the time that the application was made.

Procedure on application for review

    16.—(1)   An application for review shall be made by giving notice in Form 3 to the appropriate area committee within 14 days of the date of notification of the refusal to make a legal aid order and the applicant shall send a copy of Form 3 to the justices' clerk of the magistrates' court to which the first application for legal aid was made.

    (2)   An application under paragraph (1) shall be accompanied by the following documents—

    (a)   a copy of the completed Form 1 returned by the court under regulation 12(2); and

    (b)   a copy of the notice of refusal received under regulation 12.

    (3)   The time limit within which the application for review is to be made may, for good reason, be waived or extended by the area committee.

    (4)   The justices' clerk and the applicant shall supply such further particulars, information and documents as the area committee may require in relation to an application under paragraph (1).

Determination of review

    17.—(1)   On a review, the area committee shall consider the application for legal aid and either—

    (a)   refuse the application; or

    (b)   make a legal aid order.

    (2)   Where the area committee makes a legal aid order, it shall make a contribution order in accordance with any determination made under regulation 13.

    (3)   Where a magistrates' court or a justices' clerk has determined under regulation 13 that any legal aid order which is made shall not take effect until a contribution from disposable capital is paid, the area committee shall send the legal aid order to the appropriate justices' clerk.

    (4)   The area committee shall give notice of its decision and the reasons for it in Form 4 to—

    (a)   the applicant and his solicitor, if any, and

    (b)   the justices' clerk of the magistrates' court to which the application for legal aid was made.

    (5)   In the case of proceedings to which section 22 of the Act applies, the statement of reasons required by paragraph (4) shall comply with regulation 8(4).

8   Appealing Against a Decision to Bind Over

INTRODUCTION

A magistrates' court has power to bind over a person to keep the peace. Section 115, Magistrates' Courts Act 1980 and the Justices of the Peace Act 1861, provide a statutory basis for that power. A bind over can be imposed in addition to, or instead of, any other order.

PARTIES ENTITLED TO APPEAL

The person bound over is entitled to appeal. In the case of a parent or guardian, bound over to take proper care and exercise control over a child or young person in their care, it is the adult who has the right to appeal against the decision (s. 58(6), Criminal Justice Act 1991).

A general right of appeal lies by virtue of s. 1(1), Magistrates' Courts (Appeals from Binding Over Orders) Act 1956:

> 1(1)   Where under the Justices of the Peace Act 1361, or otherwise, a person is ordered by a magistrates' court (as defined in the Magistrates' Courts Act 1980) to enter into a recognisance with or without sureties to keep the peace or to be of good behaviour, he may appeal to the Crown Court.

PROCEDURE

The rules, as they apply to appeals against conviction and sentence, apply equally to appeals against binding over orders. The appeal is similarly by way of rehearing (Supreme Court Act 1981, s. 79(3)); however, the function of the Crown Court is to determine whether the decision reached by the magistrates was correct. In a situation therefore where the original fears had passed, but the Crown Court found they existed at the time, the appeal should not be allowed (*Hughes* v *Holley* (1988) 86 Cr App R 130, DC).

Section 1(2)(a) of the 1956 Act provides that 'the other party to the proceedings which were the occasion of the making of the order shall be the respondent to the appeal'.

In the event that no other party is able to resist the appeal then the justices themselves are able to do so (*Kent Justices, ex parte Metropolitan Police Commissioner* (1936) 100 JP 17). Similarly, where the prosecutor was bound over, the justices should appear and if appropriate state the surrounding circumstances, so far as they are not in dispute (*Preston Crown Court, ex parte Pamplin* [1981] Crim LR 338).

POWERS ON APPEAL

Section 48, Supreme Court Act 1981 applies (see Chapter 5).

9 Miscellaneous Appeals

INTRODUCTION

In addition to the main appeals against conviction and sentence, there are some lesser known appeal provisions which deal with particular areas of criminal law.
In this chapter, consideration will be given to appeals:

- by the prosecution in Customs and Excise matters;
- against declarations of relevance under the Football Spectators Act 1989;
- against decisions in respect to custody time limits.

CUSTOMS AND EXCISE PROSECUTIONS

In the case of proceedings in England or Wales, without prejudice to any right to require the statement of a case for the opinion of the High Court, the prosecutor may appeal to the Crown Court against any decision of a magistrates' court in proceedings for an offence under the Customs and Excise Acts. (Customs and Excise Management Act 1979, s. 147(3).)

This provision is far-reaching and allows the prosecution, almost unfettered, to challenge a decision of the magistrates with which they do not agree. It is almost impossible to justify this section's existence given existing remedies of judicial review and case stated.

The section is wide enough to allow a challenge to a decision relating to mode of trial, and in such circumstances the Crown Court, if it upholds the prosecution appeal, may remit the case back to the magistrates with a direction as to how to proceed (*Canterbury Crown Court, ex parte Wagstaff, The Independent*, 1 December 1997, DC).

The above appeal remedy extends to issues of sentence (*Commissioners of Customs and Excise* v *Brunt, The Times*, 25 November 1998).

CHALLENGES TO DECLARATIONS OF RELEVANCE

By virtue of the Football Spectators Act 1989, the magistrates' court can make a declaration of relevance. This certifies that a particular offence committed by the defendant was related to a football match so, for instance, being drunk and disorderly at a football ground could be so certified. The significance of the certification is that it allows the court to make additional orders on sentencing, for instance reporting to a police station at match times.

Section 108, Magistrates' Courts Act 1980 (and section 23(3), Football Spectators Act 1989) allows an appeal to lie to the Crown Court against the making of the declaration of relevance (in effect it is treated simply as a sentence that can be appealed in the usual way). It follows that if a declaration of relevance is overturned the restriction order is quashed (section 23(4), Football Spectators Act 1989).

A further appeal against the actual restriction order is provided by section 22(7), Football Spectators Act 1989:

Any person aggrieved by the decision of a magistrates' court making a restriction order under this section may appeal to the Crown Court against the decision.

CUSTODY TIME LIMITS — APPEAL ROUTES

The Prosecution of Offences Act 1985, section 22(7), (8) and (9) states:

(7) Where a magistrates' court decides to extend, or further extend, a custody or overall time limit, the accused may appeal against the decision to the Crown Court.

(8) Where a magistrates' court refuses to extend, or further extend, a custody or overall time limit, the prosecution may appeal against the refusal to the Crown Court.

(9) An appeal under subsection (8) above may not be commenced after the expiry of the limit in question; but where such an appeal is commenced before the expiry of the limit the limit shall be deemed not to have expired before the determination or abandonment of the appeal.

Quite simply this allows either party, aggrieved at the decision, to appeal. Subsection 9 is particularly important in respect of prosecution appeals, and emphasises the need to apply for an extension in good time. Waiting until the day of expiry is now to be discouraged as it will not allow time for an appeal to be lodged. It will be a rare case when the Crown Court appeal route is not used. One must always remember that the availability of other remedies is a factor when consideration is being given as to whether to grant leave to apply for judicial review. An appeal by way of case stated is not available in respect of interlocutory ruling.

Procedure

Application is made by letter, the date of hearing being arranged in advance with the listing officer. It is a matter for the judge whether evidence is heard or the matter is considered on representations alone (*Crown Court at Norwich, ex parte Parker and Ward* (1993) 96 Cr App R 68, DC). It is then simply a matter for the judge to decide whether to extend the time limit or admit the defendant to bail. The specific procedural requirements are set out in the Crown Court Rules 1982, r. 27A.

Appeals relating to time limits

27A—(1) This rule applies—

(a) to any appeal brought by an accused, under subsection (7) of section 22 of the Prosecution of Offences Act 1985, against a decision of a magistrates' court to extend, or further extend, a time limit imposed by regulations made under subsection (1) of that section; and

(b) to any appeal brought by the prosecution, under subsection (8) of the said section 22, against a decision of a magistrates' court to refuse to extend, or further extend, such a time limit.

(2) An appeal to which this rule applies shall be commenced by the appellant's giving notice in writing of appeal—

(a) to the clerk to the magistrates' court which took the decision;

(b) if the appeal is brought by the accused, to the prosecutor and, if the prosecution is to be carried on by the Crown Prosecution Service, to the appropriate Crown Prosecutor;

(c) if the appeal is brought by the prosecution, to the accused; and

(d) to the appropriate officer of the Crown Court.

(3) The notice of an appeal to which this rule applies shall state the date on which the time limit applicable to the case is due to expire and, if the appeal is brought by the accused under section 22(7) of the Prosecution of Offences Act 1985, the date on which the time limit would have expired had the court decided not to extend or further extend the time limit.

(4) On receiving notice of an appeal to which this rule applies, the appropriate officer of the Crown Court shall enter the appeal and give notice of the time and place of the hearing to—

(a) the appellant;

(b) the other party to the appeal; and

(c) the clerk to the magistrates' court which took the decision.

(5) Without prejudice to the power of the Crown Court to give leave for an appeal to be abandoned, an appellant may abandon an appeal to which this rule applies by giving notice in writing to any person to whom notice of the appeal was required to be given by paragraph (2) not later than the third day preceding the day fixed for the hearing of the appeal:

Provided that, for the purpose of determining whether notice was properly given in accordance with this paragraph, there shall be disregarded any Saturday and Sunday and any day which is specified to be a bank holiday in England and Wales under section 1(1) of the Banking and Financial Dealings Act 1971.

Further Appeal

Both judicial review and case stated is available, the latter being the preferred option in most cases, as it allows the factual basis for the judge's decision to be put before the High Court (*Central Criminal Court, ex parte Behbehani* [1994] Crim LR 352, DC).

A final caution against delaying the application to extend is sounded by the decision in *Croydon Crown Court, ex parte Commissioners of Customs and Excise* [1997] 8 Archbold News 1, DC, which states that the High Court has no power to intervene once the original limit has expired.

10   Judicial Review

INTRODUCTION

Judicial review, as the words imply, is not an appeal from a decision, but a review of the manner in which the decision was made. (*Chief Constable of North Wales Police* v *Evans* [1982] 1 WLR 1155.)

Judicial review is the process by which decisions of magistrates' courts and Crown Courts (except where concerned with matters relating to trial on indictment) are 'moved' to the Divisional Court of the Queen's Bench Division of the High Court for scrutiny.

The High Court is concerned with the way the decision was made, not the merits of the decision. It is the way in which the High Court exercises control over inferior tribunals, which includes both magistrates' courts and Crown Courts acting in their appellate capacity.

Judicial review is not a static concept, and has shown itself able to adapt to meet changing needs and circumstances. It must, however, be distinguished from appeal and will not develop into an appeal remedy (see *Carlisle Crown Court, ex parte Marcus-Moore, The Times*, 26 October 1981, a case in which fresh evidence came to light, but there was no complaint in respect to the Crown Court appeal itself and so relief was denied).

Any decision of the magistrates' court is amenable to judicial review and practitioners must be alert at all times to the possibility of a challenge.

After every decision, whether an adjournment, or a consideration of a legal or some other matter, the advocate should ask whether the decision was made lawfully. If not, judicial review should be explored.

OVERLAP OF REMEDIES

The availability of judicial review only serves to cloud the process of appeal and review. We will see that its purpose is greatly different from case stated, but also that there is an overlap. What is the best course where there has been a procedural irregularity or where bias has been shown? Should one simply appeal to the Crown Court for a fair hearing, or seek judicial review? If judicial review were refused, would the Crown Court appeal still be open? Would it be out of time? Should you appeal to the Crown Court and ask for proceedings to be adjourned pending the outcome of the judicial review?

All of the above questions need careful consideration, and the main one, i.e. the availability of Crown Court appeal and judicial review (in rare cases), has only recently been answered.

The *Rowlands* Case

In *Hereford Magistrates' Court, ex parte Rowlands, The Times*, 17 February 1997, the Divisional Court considered a number of conjoined appeals. Rowlands had been denied an adjournment to call two witnesses critical to the defence. Accordingly he claimed the proceedings were unfair. At this juncture three remedies were seemingly available:

- an appeal against conviction to the Crown Court;
- an appeal by way of case stated;
- judicial review.

The question arose as to whether the appropriate remedy was simply an appeal to the Crown Court, which would have had the effect of remedying the unfairness. However, this would not have remedied the unfairness of the original hearing.

An appeal by way of case stated (on the grounds that the decision was wrong in law, the justices having departed from well-known principles of justice and procedure) would have had the effect of stopping an appeal to the Crown Court, so if it had been unsuccessful, it would have left the defendant convicted.

Judicial review is said to be available only when all other avenues are exhausted, so therefore it might well have been thought that one must always exercise an appeal to the Crown Court first. This objection arose as a result of the court's decision in *Peterborough Magistrates' Court, ex parte Dowler, The Times*, 24 May 1996.

The court in *Rowlands* resolved the issue and stated the following:

It was not doubted that *Dowler* was correctly decided but the decision was not to be treated as authority that a party complaining of procedural unfairness or bias in the magistrates' court should be denied leave to move for judicial review and left to whatever rights he might have in the Crown Court.

So to hold would be to emasculate the long-established supervisory jurisdiction of the Divisional Court over magistrates' courts, which had over the years proved an invaluable guarantee of the integrity of proceedings in those courts.

The crucial role of the magistrates' courts made it more important that jurisdiction should be retained with a view to ensuring that the high standards of fairness and impartiality were maintained.

Two notes of caution should be sounded:

● Leave to move should not be granted unless the applicant advanced an apparently plausible complaint which, if made good, might arguably be held to vitiate the proceedings in the magistrates' court.

Immaterial and minor deviations from best principles would not have that effect and the court should be respectful of discretionary decisions of magistrates' courts as of all other courts. The Divisional Court should be slow to intervene, and should do so only where good, or arguably good grounds were shown.

● The decision whether to grant relief by way of judicial review was a discretionary one. Many factors might properly influence the exercise of discretion and it would be foolish and impossible to anticipate them all. The need for the applicant to make full disclosure of all matters relevant to the exercise of discretion should require no emphasis. However, the existence of a right of appeal to the Crown Court, particularly if unexercised, should not ordinarily weigh against the grant of leave to move, or of substantive relief in a proper case.

The Way Forward

In light of the above, where it is alleged that the justices acted unfairly or in excess of jurisdiction, in appropriate cases both appeal and judicial review might be available. In such cases appellants are advised to take the following course of action:

● lodge an immediate appeal with the Crown Court, asking that the case be adjourned until the outcome of the judicial review;
● apply, without delay, for judicial review, making clear in the application that the above steps have been taken;
● if the Crown Court shows reluctance to delay the hearing of the case, apply to the Divisional Court for the Crown Court proceedings to be stayed.

A similar dilemma arises in respect of case stated, but is aggravated by the fact that an application to state a case precludes a Crown Court appeal. Unless the appellant is certain that the justices erred in law, it is almost always better to appeal first to the Crown Court. That way there is a rehearing on facts and law, and if the appellant remains convicted, any legal point can still be appealed by way of case stated from the Crown Court.

GROUNDS FOR JUDICIAL REVIEW

The grounds are that the magistrates' court or Crown Court has:

● exceeded or abused its powers, or made an error in law (illegality);
● breached the rules of natural justice or other established procedures and rules (procedural impropriety), which would include abuse of process;

- reached a decision which no reasonable tribunal, properly directed and on the evidence, could have reached (irrationality).

Any one of the above will suffice. However, it cannot be emphasised enough that judicial review is a *discretionary* remedy, and not every failing will be justiciable. The words quoted above from *Rowlands* should be considered very carefully, and advocates are reminded of their own duties to the court, particularly if asked for assistance. Many books describe the heads of judicial review in different ways, and it is true to say that the heads overlap. In addition each head can be further broken down, so we begin to look at topics such as 'taking irrelevant factors into account' and 'bias', as sub-heads.

ILLEGALITY

The magistrates' court and Crown Court are creatures of statute. Their powers are derived from Parliament and they must exercise them according to the terms of the statute. Acting outside those powers or with no power at all is illegal and of no effect.

Practically, however, the court may purport to exercise a power, and if such an exercise is left uncorrected a grave injustice can occur. Equally, refusing to exercise jurisdiction may give rise to judicial review, where for example the justices refuse to allow a rehearing because the applicant arrived late at court.

Example

Consider the case where a magistrates' court passes a sentence of seven months' custody on a 22-year-old man who has pleaded guilty to common assault. Assuming that this is the only offence, and no licence period has been revoked, this is in excess of the magistrates' court's powers of sentencing, which in this case are limited to six months' imprisonment. This decision is on the face of it amenable to judicial review. However, consider whether the appropriate remedy is: (a) to invite the magistrates to reopen the sentence after reminding them of their maximum powers; or (b) failing that, an appeal to the Crown Court.

In cases similar to the above example, the Divisional Court has consistently said that a sentence should only be judicially reviewed if it falls clearly outside the broad area of the lower court's discretion (*Truro Crown Court, ex parte Adair* [1997] COD 296, DC). In the above example, not only does it fall outside the discretion, but it is clearly beyond the court's powers.

In this case the most appropriate remedy would be to appeal to the Crown Court against sentence.

When exercising its powers, the court must take into account all relevant considerations, and ignore irrelevant ones. To do otherwise would be to exercise the available powers improperly, and accordingly not lawfully.

Example

The prosecution were not able to adduce evidence vital to their case. However, an imminent change in the law would allow for the admissibility of the same evidence. Accordingly, the justices allowed an adjournment for that new law to come into effect. The Divisional Court held that the future change in the law was an irrelevant consideration (*Walsall Justices, ex parte W* [1990] 1 QB 253).

Discretion is there to be exercised and any fettering of it may well be unlawful. General policies are allowed, but each case must be considered on its merits. For example, legal aid will not generally be granted to contest a 'no-insurance' matter, but what if the driver is the sole carer for a severely handicapped child, and that child's only means of transport?

Powers must only be exercised by those authorised to exercise them. A court clerk has no place in the decision making process as it relates to the finding of fact; nor does a magistrates' court have power, during a pre-trial review, to order the defence to disclose their case (despite the protestations of many clerks).

IRRATIONALITY

This head, also described as '*Wednesbury* unreasonableness', is the one that will most frequently give rise to challenge. It also encompasses decision making which involves 'bad faith' or 'improper motives'.

Meaning

The classic test is whether the decision is one 'which no tribunal, properly directed on the evidence, could have reached'. The test is imprecise and largely subjective, nevertheless practitioners need to be alert to its use, as the courts have shown themselves to be remarkably flexible in its use.

Example

A refusal to grant legal aid to a 16-year-old charged with obstructing a police officer in the execution of his duty, was quashed as being irrational. The expertise required for the cross-examination of a police officer, and for proofing defence witnesses, was beyond that of a 16-year-old (*Scunthorpe Justices, ex parte S, The Times*, 5 March 1998, DC).

Care must be taken in respect of sentencing decisions, as appeal avenues should be carefully explored first. There seems no reason, however, why a prosecutor could not seek judicial review of an irrational sentence, as there is no alternative appeal.

PROCEDURAL IMPROPRIETY

Proceedings must be conducted not only lawfully but fairly as well. The principles of natural justice need to be adhered to.

The court must ensure that a defendant has notice of the allegations against him or her, is allowed to present the case properly, and that there is no appearance of bias. A court's decision must accord with any legitimate expectations given, and a court must, in some instances, give reasons for its decision.

Example

A solicitor criticised the listing practice of the court and was dealt with for contempt. No opportunity was given for the solicitor to seek advice and representation before the issue was decided. The court held this to be unfair (note however that there is not an *absolute* right to legal representation) (*Tamworth Magistrates' Court, ex parte Walsh* [1994] COD 277).

SUMMARY

The heads of judicial review are both detailed and confusing. A perusal of the standard works in the area will only serve to reveal even more irregularity in this area of law. As a guideline, if the decision 'feels wrong' then it is worthy of further investigation. Clearly there is no substitute for knowing inside out the courts' powers in all the areas of criminal practice — it is somewhat astounding the actions which courts undertake, believing them to be lawful, only later to be challenged when the mistake is spotted. The Divisional Court is consistently reminding advocates of their duty to ensure that the court is assisted with procedural advice where appropriate.

WHO MAY APPLY FOR JUDICIAL REVIEW?

The applicant must have 'standing'. For the purposes of this text, both the prosecution and defence will have sufficient standing in any decision of the court relating to the case in which they are involved.

The Crown Prosecution Service have shown themselves more willing in recent years to seek judicial review in appropriate cases. No longer are the defence able to sit back with confidence when a decision has been taken in their favour, which they themselves know to be more than generous.

Example

A magistrates' court, offer considering mode of trial accepted jurisdiction in respect of a burglary at a dormitory at a boy's boarding school, at night, when the boys were present. In this case the defence had represented the case suitable for summary trial. The CPS applied for judicial review of the decision and it was quashed. The matter was remitted to the justices (*Stamford Magistrates' Court, ex parte DPP* [1998] COD 10, DC). This decision may be contrasted with the following case, which illustrates the discretionary nature of judicial review. Interestingly the court commented on the fact that the defence had been blameless (unlike in the above case) and that the CPS had not brought the National Mode of Trial guidelines to the attention of the court, nor had the CPS sought an adjournment after the decision in order to take immediate judicial review proceedings. In *Horseferry Road Magistrates' Court, ex parte DPP* [1997] COD 89, DC, the court accepted jurisdiction in respect of an offence of possessing 114 Ecstasy tablets with intent to supply. The defendant was sentenced to a financial penalty which at the time of the judicial review had been paid. The court quashed the decision but did not remit the case to the magistrates' court.

JUDICIAL REVIEW OF ACQUITTALS

If a court convicts unfairly, judicial review lies, but what if the acquittal was unfair? An error of law will allow the prosecution to seek an appeal by way of case stated, but what of the situation where there is a breach of natural justice which affects the prosecution case?

The basic rule is that a man must not be put at risk of conviction twice; this is the rule against double jeopardy. However, where a decision to acquit can be said to be a nullity, in effect no decision at all, judicial review will lie.

What is not clear, however, is whether a breach of the rules of natural justice necessarily makes the proceedings a nullity: this leaves the prosecution in some difficulty. In respect of successful appeals against conviction in the Crown Court, it would appear that in some cases judicial review will lie, as there is no double jeopardy (see below).

The leading case of *Harrington v Roots* [1984] 2 All ER 481, HL, sought to clarify the position. In this case the prosecution at date of trial sought an adjournment which was granted. The defence then asked for an alternative adjournment date, due to the fact that the defendant was on holiday on the new date. The justices refused to allocate a new date, and without any reference to the prosecution as to whether they were able to proceed forthwith, decided to dismiss the charges. The defence accepted that there had been a breach of natural justice in that the prosecution were not given an opportunity to present their case, but submitted that the decision to dismiss the informations amounted to an acquittal, and accordingly judicial review was not available. The House of Lords moved away from the question of natural justice and was able to determine that the court had acted outside its statutory duty. Accordingly the decision was a nullity. The House of Lords went on to say that:

> My Lords, I have already at the outset of this speech drawn attention to the use of the phrase 'breach of the rules of natural justice' in the judgment of Robert Goff LJ and in the certificate and I have already indicated that I did not think that such a breach was for present purposes the relevant consideration. My reasons for so thinking will now be apparent. It is not difficult to visualise a case, though I hope it would be extremely rare, where justices acting within their jurisdiction nevertheless acted so unfairly that they could properly be said to be acting in breach of the rules of natural justice. I would not wish it to be thought in such a

case that, if an acquittal followed, that acquittal was for that reason alone necessarily susceptible to judicial review. In my view the test is not breach of the rules of natural justice but whether the decision of the justices to dismiss an information is a decision which they had no jurisdiction to take because they were declining to adjudicate on a matter on which it was their duty to adjudicate and thus was a nullity. On this basis, to raise the correct question the certificate should be treated as amended so that it reads: 'Whether, on the dismissal by the justices of an information after they have failed or refused to adjudicate thereupon by declining to receive the evidence desired to be led by the prosecution, the Queen's Bench Divisional Court has power on an application by the prosecutor for judicial review to quash the acquittal and remit the matter to the justices for rehearing.' My Lords, I would answer that amended question in the affirmative on the ground that that dismissal was a nullity (save that in most such cases I do not think it would be necessary for certiorari to issue as well as mandamus).

Result

It would appear therefore that a 'simple' breach of natural justice does not allow the prosecutor to judicially review an acquittal gained in the magistrates' court.

The Crown Court Position

A few days after the *Harrington* judgment, the House of Lords delivered its speeches in the case of *Weight* v *MacKay* [1984] 2 All ER 678, HL. The question which was certified for answer by their Lordships was amended from its original form, and read in substance the same as in *Harrington*. Accordingly if the Crown Court failed to hear an appeal on its merits by declining to receive all the admissible evidence desired to be led by the respondent, judicial review may lie. However, in this case, the hearing could certainly not be said to have been a nullity, and it is clear that there had been a breach of natural justice by not allowing the Crown to present its case properly. It is regrettable that the point originally certified was not answered, as that would have cleared up once and for all the question of when acquittals can be judicially reviewed.

Arguably, the prosecution can judicially review successful appeals against conviction at the Crown Court. The reasoning behind this argument is that, as the court pointed out in *Weight* v *MacKay*, there is no double jeopardy. If the decision were to be quashed the appellant would only stand convicted of the offence which was tried in the magistrates' court, on the one occasion on which they were put in peril of conviction.

It will be up to a future court, on clear facts amounting to a breach of natural justice, to resolve the point. Clearly though, there is much scope for argument that in Crown Court proceedings (but almost certainly not in summary ones), a breach of the rules of natural justice is judicially reviewable, just as in the case of fraud in the Crown Court.

This situation is somewhat biased towards the defence, but it seems that even where an acquittal has been obtained by fraud in summary proceedings, judicial review will not lie, due to the overriding precedence of the double jeopardy rule.

REMEDIES AVAILABLE

● Certiorari   This order has the effect of quashing the decision complained of.
● Mandamus   An order requiring the inferior body to perform a specified act or duty.
● Prohibition   An order to direct a body to cease acting or continuing to act in a way inconsistent with its jurisdiction.
● Declaration   A statement of the legal rights of the applicant.
● Variation of sentence   See below.
● Stay of proceedings   As an alternative to remitting the matter for reconsideration, the court may order the stay of proceedings.

In addition the court can grant injunctions and also award damages.

PRACTICAL EFFECT OF JUDICIAL REVIEW

In respect of a conviction the court will generally quash the original conviction, and in most cases order a retrial. In respect of other orders the court will similarly direct the court to reconsider them afresh, or to do something they have so far not done, whether through ignorance or choice. The power to stay proceedings (on the grounds of abuse of process or other grounds) will be used sparingly and only in clear cases.

One should not assume, however, that the result will be different; it may well be the case that even if the matter is properly adjudicated upon, the result will be the same. In cases where the court is invited to quash a sentence, the court has power to substitute a sentence itself, without remitting the matter to the justices (Supreme Court Act 1981, s. 43(1)).

MAKING THE APPLICATION — PROCEDURAL POINTS

The Supreme Court Act 1981, ss. 29, 31 and RSC Ord. 53 detail the procedure to be followed:

● Standing   It is essential that the party seeking to challenge a decision has the necessary standing (RSC Ord. 53, r. 3(7)).
● Delay   The application must be made promptly, and in any event within three months of the making of the decision being complained about (RSC Ord. 53, r. 4(1)). The importance of this rule cannot be over-emphasised, and practitioners must be aware that three months is the maximum, but in any event the complaint must be made promptly. The mere fact that the complaint was made within three months does not preclude the possibility of leave being refused on account of undue delay in

making the application (*Brighton and Hove Magistrates, ex parte Clarke* [1997] 5 Archbold News 3, DC). The court will need evidence to show that progress was made, and applicants are advised to note fully the dates of legal aid applications, briefs to Counsel and the reason for any delay. Such information should appear in the supporting affidavit. An application to extend the time limit can be made to the court, but there must be very good grounds for the court doing so (RSC Ord. 53, r. 4(1)).

● Leave   The leave of the court must be granted. An applicant will need to show an arguable case for judicial review.
● Bail   The High Court has the power to grant bail, pursuant to RSC Ord. 79. See the earlier chapter on bail appeals for details of the application procedure.
● Suspension of disqualification   Road Traffic Offenders Act 1988, s. 40(5) allows the High Court to suspend the disqualification. A request should be pleaded in the Notice of Application made to the court.
● Alternative remedies must be exhausted   Following *Rowlands* (above), this now has less significance for the criminal law practitioner, but heed the caution given in respect of minor deviations from good practice. Generally excessive sentences should be appealed to the Crown Court, before judicial review is considered.
● The question for the court must be real   It will not grant relief if the result is of no practical effect, or the answer purely academic.
● Legal aid   The court has no power to grant legal aid, an application needs to be made to the Legal Aid Board Area Office in the usual way. The *Legal Aid Handbook* indicates that in deciding whether to grant legal aid, the issue for the board is primarily whether the tangible advantage to be gained for the applicant justifies the cost of the proceedings, rather than whether there is a general public interest in the decision under review being challenged. It is also suggested that in all cases the proposed respondent should be given prior notice of the intended proceedings.
● There are a number of practice directions which deal with procedural points, including the preparation of case bundles. It is vital that they are followed to the letter. The main directions are highlighted below.

THE APPLICATION PROCEDURE

It will be no surprise that the rules in relation to the application procedure are detailed. In order to maximise the chances of success it is vital to follow them to the letter and to forward to the Crown Office an application which supplies the Court with the maximum information possible. The rules and precedents are reproduced below.

LEAVE

The first stage is to apply, ex parte, for leave. A standard notice of application (Form 86A) together with the grounds of the application should be sent to the Crown Office. All applications should be supported by an affidavit. Order 53, r. 3(2) states that an application for leave should be filed by notice in Form 86A containing a statement of:

- the name and description of the applicant;
- the relief sought and the grounds upon which the application is sought;
- the name and address of the applicant's solicitors, if any;
- the applicant's address for service.

In addition the notice must be supported by an affidavit verifying the facts relied upon.

The notice of application should be fully supported by any authority relied upon. Authorities known to the applicant, but contrary to the case, should be cited and distinguished if at all possible.

It is vital that the applicant's case is pleaded as fully as possible. Cases are often won or lost at this vital stage, and the applicant will generally be at an advantage as the application is considered ex parte on paper.

Role of the Respondent

An ex parte application on paper does not preclude the respondent from making representations. Since a letter before action will have been sent in almost all cases, this is an opportunity for the respondent to answer, early on, the applicant's case. Clearly, oral representations cannot be made, but the respondent can place written representations before the court. This procedure is particularly useful when the respondent is arguing that the applicant's application is misguided for some reason. Order 53, r. 6 details the requirements to provide the other party with copy documents.

Oral Applications

The court of its own motion, or the applicant in the notice of application, can request an oral hearing. Applicants should generally avoid such a course of action since it will only delay the granting of leave, and give the respondent a chance to respond and possibly defeat the application at an early stage. However, where interlocutory relief is required, an oral hearing should be requested. It is a matter for the respondent whether or not to attend. Order 53, r. 6(4) details the requirements of the respondent to serve affidavits relied upon.

In complicated matters the court is becoming more proactive in ordering oral hearings.

Decision

The judge can either grant or refuse leave to apply for judicial review. If leave is refused the applicant can, within 10 days of being served with notification of refusal of leave, renew the application to the Divisional Court. Form 86B is used for this purpose. The appeal will be by way of an oral hearing, see Ord. 53, r. 3(4)(a). Extensions of time can be granted in appropriate cases (Ord. 3, r. 5).

PROCEDURE POST LEAVE

Once leave is granted the applicant has 14 days to serve a notice of motion in Form 86, along with a copy of the order granting leave. Such documents are to be served on all persons affected and the Crown Office, along with an affidavit of service.

Respondent's Affidavit

If the respondent wishes to respond, an affidavit in reply may be served. The respondent should notify the Crown Office of the intention to do so, and it should be served as soon as reasonably practicable and in any event within 56 days. The respondent has the right to be present and represented at the hearing.

Reconsideration of Applicant's case

Once evidence for the respondent has been served, the applicant has a duty to reconsider the merits of the case. It is at this point that the applicant may consider amending the notice or serving additional affidavits (with leave).

THE HEARING

The Crown Office list is divided into five parts. *Practice Direction (Crown Office List)* [1987] 1 WLR 232, details the main constituent parts. It is important that applicants and respondents follow the instructions contained in the *Practice Direction*, to ensure the smooth running of the court.

Part B of the list details cases ready to be heard. At this point the court will issue an 'active case letter' to the applicant. The applicant must reply within 14 days confirming that the case is still active and ready to be heard. If the applicant fails to respond, the case will automatically be listed for hearing and the applicant will have to show cause why the matter should not be struck out for want of prosecution.

At this point the directions in *Practice Direction (Crown Office List: Preparation for Hearings)* [1994] 1 WLR 1551 and *Practice Direction (Evidence: Documents)* [1983] 1 WLR 922, come into operation. These require a paginated and indexed bundle of documents and a skeleton argument to be lodged, within five days of the date of hearing. The respondent must produce a skeleton argument within three days of the date of hearing.

Consent Orders

Practice Direction (Crown Office List: Uncontested Proceedings) [1983] 1 WLR 925 gave effect to consent orders in criminal causes by extending the principles originally set out in *Practice Direction (Crown Office List: Uncontested Proceedings)* [1982] 1 WLR 979, to criminal matters. The practice directions, reproduced at the end of this chapter, should be read in conjunction with each other.

A Full Hearing

If the case is not settled by consent, the matter will proceed to a full hearing. The usual principles relating to costs apply.

Appearance of Justices

Unless the bona fides or character of a justice of the peace has been called into question it is not usual for them to appear. They may, however, file affidavits. Any appearance by justices may make them liable to costs. The court may require justices to appear. In such instances the clerk to the justices should consult with the Treasury Solicitor.

FURTHER APPEALS

There is no appeal to the Court of Appeal in criminal matters. The only remaining remedy is by way of appeal to the House of Lords, if the Divisional Court certifies a point of general public importance, or if the House of Lords itself grants leave.

JUDICIAL REVIEW — CASE STUDY

Facts

On 12 June 1998, Mr Matthew Brown was arrested for an offence of common assault, contrary to section 39, Criminal Justice Act 1988. He was charged with the offence, and bailed to appear before Wigan Magistrates' Court on 19 June 1998. On that date, he pleaded not guilty to the offence, and the matter was set down for trial, two hours being set aside, on 10 July 1998. Mr Brown indicated that he would be calling three witnesses in his defence, and would be seeking to obtain video evidence from a closed circuit television camera, situated near to the scene of the alleged assault.

The matter proceeded to trial on 10 July 1998, the prosecution calling its sole witness, PC Hammer. The prosecution opened its case on the basis that at around 12 noon, PC Hammer had seen the defendant acting 'suspiciously' near to a BMW motor vehicle. The officer approached the defendant and asked, 'what are you doing?'. The defendant replied, 'what the fuck's it got to do with you?'. PC Hammer warned Brown as to his future conduct and asked him to empty his pockets. Brown refused and stated that, 'you've no right to do that'. The officer then goes on to say that Brown raised his right fist, and punched him in the face, before running off. The officer gave chase, and apprehended Brown a few minutes later. Brown was arrested and conveyed to Wigan police station. When interviewed under caution, Brown denied the assault.

PC Hammer gave evidence in the above terms and was cross-examined by Brown.

During cross-examination, Brown put the following proposition to PC Hammer, 'It's right, isn't it Mr Hammer, that I did not punch you, and that you have made this up because you didn't like my tone?'

PC Hammer replied, 'Are you calling me a liar?'. To which Brown replied, 'Just answer my question please'.

At this point the chairman of the bench said the following to Brown, 'Mr Brown, you must learn to control yourself. In my court we do not accept that police officers make evidence up for such poor reasons, and we will not tolerate you accusing PC Hammer of lying. Do you have anything else to ask?'.

Brown replied that he had no further questions.

The Crown closed its case, and Brown gave evidence in his own defence.

Brown alleged that he had been split up from his group of friends and was somewhat lost. He was not acting suspiciously and had not noticed the BMW. He accepted the officer's version of events, save that he did not assault the officer, and could only conclude that the officer was trying to 'save face', when confronted with a young man who was not going to be intimidated by the excessive powers of the executive's lackeys. This account was maintained in cross-examination.

At the end of his evidence, Brown indicated that he wished to call his three witnesses, at which point the chairman stated, 'Mr Brown, we have heard enough of this nonsense. Your allegation against this officer is pure fantasy on your part and there is nothing more you or anyone else could say to convince my colleagues and

me otherwise. We find you guilty of this offence. [Antecedent information given by
the prosecutor.] We note that you have had a number of custodial sentences in the
past — a sorry record for a man of only 25 years of age. It would seem that you are
violent and unable to accept responsibility for your actions. We will not tolerate your
kind in this town, and take the view that this offence is so serious that only a custodial
sentence is appropriate — we do not need reports. You will go to prison for nine
months'.

Mr Brown wishes to challenge the decision.

The following documents reflect the pleadings in the above matter.

Solution

Consider other remedies, particularly in relation to sentence. However, other
remedies are not appropriate in this case, as a Crown Court appeal could not remedy
the breach of natural justice.

(1)   Mr Brown instructs solicitors who request a reopening of the matter.
(2)   No reply received from the court.
(3)   Notice of judicial review and affidavit in support.
(4)   Consent order (assuming in this case that the respondents, after reflection,
concede that the hearing was unfair and the sentence unlawful).

Upon the consent order being allowed, it would be up to the High Court to decide
whether to remit the matter to the magistrates' court for a trial by a different bench.

In such cases it is likely that the Crown Prosecution Service would also be an
interested party.

IN THE HIGH COURT OF JUSTICE

QUEEN'S BENCH DIVISION

CROWN OFFICE LIST   CO/_____

In the matter of an application by Matthew Brown for leave to apply for judicial review (Ord. 53, r. 3).

THE QUEEN

—v—

WIGAN MAGISTRATES' COURT

Ex parte Matthew Brown

Applicant's reference no.	Crown Office reference no.

This form must be read together with Notes of Guidance obtainable from the Crown Office.

To the Master of the Crown Office, Royal Courts of Justice, Strand, London WC2A 2LL.

Name, address and description of applicant.

Mr Matthew Brown, 184 Apple Road, Wigan WN6. Surveyor.

Judgment, order, decision or other proceedings in respect of which relief is sought:

A decision of justices sitting at Wigan Magistrates' Court on 10 July 1998 to convict the applicant of common assault contrary to section 39, Criminal Justice Act 1988, and a sentence of nine months' imprisonment.

RELIEF SOUGHT

(1)   Certiorari to quash the conviction. Further or alternatively,
(2)   Certiorari to quash the said sentence. Further or alternatively,
(3)   Variation of sentence pursuant to the Supreme Court Act 1981, s. 43.
(4)   The applicant further seeks: (i) bail under RSC Ord. 79, (ii) an expedited hearing if leave is granted.

Name and address of applicant's solicitors or, if no solicitors acting, the address for service of the applicant.	Messrs FREE M and Co. 1 The Parade Wigan WN1 1AB

Signed.................................... Dated......................................

GROUNDS ON WHICH RELIEF IS SOUGHT

(1)   The applicant is a surveyor, employed by the Amity Partnership, High Street, Wigan WN6 1AB.

(2)   On 12 June 1998 the applicant was arrested by Police Constable Hammer of the Greater Manchester Police, for an offence of common assault, contrary to section 39, Criminal Justice Act 1988.

(3)   On 19 June 1998, the matter was set down for trial, the applicant having indicated that he would be calling three witnesses in his defence, and would attempt to obtain video evidence of the incident. The matter was listed for two hours. The applicant was unrepresented.

(4)   On 10 July 1998, the matter proceeded to trial. The case was opened by the Crown on the following basis: that at around 12 noon, PC Hammer had seen the defendant acting 'suspiciously' near to a BMW motor vehicle. The officer approached the defendant and asked, 'what are you doing?'. The defendant replied, 'what the fuck's it got to do with you?'. PC Hammer warned Brown as to his future conduct and asked him to empty his pockets. Brown refused and stated that, 'you've no right to do that'. The officer then goes on to say that Brown raised his right fist, and punched him in the face, before running off. The officer gave chase, and apprehended Brown a few minutes later. Brown was arrested and conveyed to Wigan police station. When interviewed under caution, Brown denied the assault.

The Crown called one witness, namely PC Hammer. During cross-examination the following exchange took place:

Brown: 'It's right, isn't it Mr Hammer, that I did not punch you, and that you have made this up because you didn't like my tone?'
PC Hammer: 'Are you calling me a liar?'
Brown: 'Just answer my question please.'
Chairman of the Bench: 'Mr Brown, you must learn to control yourself. In my court we do not accept that police officers make evidence up for such poor reasons, and we will not tolerate you accusing PC Hammer of lying. Do you have anything else to ask?'
Brown: 'No, I have no further questions.'

(5)   The Crown called no further evidence.

(6)   The applicant gave evidence in his own defence.

(7)   The applicant indicated that he wished to call his three witnesses to give evidence, at which point the chairman of the bench stated the following: 'Mr Brown, we have heard enough of this nonsense. Your allegation against this officer is pure fantasy on your part and there is nothing more you or anyone else could say to convince my colleagues and me otherwise. We find you guilty of this offence. [Antecedent information given by the prosecutor.] We note that you have had a number of custodial sentences in the past — a sorry record for a man of only 25 years of age. It would seem that you are violent and unable to accept responsibility for your

actions. We will not tolerate your kind in this town, and take the view that this offence is so serious that only a custodial sentence is appropriate — we do not need reports. You will go to prison for nine months.'

(8)   A committal warrant was issued.

(9)   The applicant contends that the chairman of the bench acted unlawfully/in breach of natural justice in that he was denied the opportunity to call evidence in his defence. Further or alternatively that the chairman of the bench displayed bias toward the applicant and favour toward the police officer.

(10)   Further, that the sentence of nine months' imprisonment passed was unlawful in that the maximum sentence in respect of this offence is one of six months' imprisonment.

Legal Propositions

The maximum sentence in respect of common assault is six months' imprisonment (s. 39, CJA 1988).

As a matter of natural justice the applicant has a right to be heard and call witnesses.

APPLICANT'S AFFIDAVIT IN SUPPORT

Deponent: Matthew Brown
First Affidavit
Filed on behalf of the
Applicant.
Sworn:_____

CO/_____

IN THE HIGH COURT OF JUSTICE

QUEEN'S BENCH DIVISION

CROWN OFFICE LIST

In the matter of an application by Matthew Brown for leave to apply for judicial review (Ord. 53, r. 3).

THE QUEEN

—v—

WIGAN MAGISTRATES' COURT

Ex parte Matthew Brown

AFFIDAVIT

I, Matthew Brown, of Her Majesty's Prison Manchester, Surveyor, MAKE OATH and say as follows:

1.   I am the applicant and make this affidavit in support of my application herein for leave to apply for judicial review of a conviction for common assault and sentence of nine months' imprisonment passed upon me by the Wigan Magistrates' Court on 10 July 1998.

2.   Save as stated herein all the facts and matters hereinafter deposed to are within my knowledge, information and belief.

3.   I have read a copy of the Notice of Application (Form 86A) and I confirm that the factual assertions contained therein are true.

4.   There is now produced and shown to me marked 'MB/1' a copy of the memorandum of conviction and sentence passed relevant to this application.

5.   I am advised by my solicitor and believe that my conviction was unfair and that there are no continued grounds for my detention. I invite this Honourable Court to grant me immediate bail.

Sworn etc . . .

CONSENT ORDER — UNCONTESTED CRIMINAL PROCEEDINGS

<u>IN THE HIGH COURT OF JUSTICE</u>   CO/ _____

<u>QUEEN'S BENCH DIVISION</u>

<u>CROWN OFFICE LIST</u>

In the matter of an application by Matthew Brown for judicial review.

THE QUEEN

—v—

WIGAN MAGISTRATES' COURT

Ex parte Matthew Brown

The applicant and the respondent do hereby consent, subject to the approval of the court, to an order that the conviction and sentence passed by the justices sitting at Wigan Magistrates' Court on 10 July 1998, be brought up and quashed and that the respondent do pay the costs of the applicant on a full indemnity basis.

The reason for the making of the said order is that (a) on reflection the justices acknowledge that the comments made during trial were inappropriate and may be construed as showing favouritism towards the police, (b) that the defendant has a right to call witnesses in his defence when they were present at Court, (c) the sentence of nine months' imprisonment was one which the justices had no power to pass.

....
Signed for applicant   Signed for respondent

DATED: _____

THE CROWN OFFICE LIST

NOTES FOR GUIDANCE

APPLICATIONS FOR JUDICIAL REVIEW

GENERAL

These notes, issued at the direction of the Lord Chief Justice, are not intended to be exhaustive but merely to offer an outline of the procedure to be followed. Applicants and their legal advisers should consult Order 53 of the Rules of the Supreme Court as amended by S.I. 1980 No. 2000 for a full account.

1   LEGAL AID

Neither the Court nor the Crown Office has power to grant legal aid which may only be obtained from the Legal Aid Board. Application should be made to the appropriate Area Office whose address will be found in the telephone directory, or through a Solicitor, who may advise as to such an application for the Committee's consideration, under the Green Form Scheme.

2   TIME

(a)   Applications for leave to apply for Judicial Review must be made as soon as possible after the date of the judgment order, decision or other proceeding in respect of which relief is sought but in any event within the period of three months allowed by Order 53 rule 4.

(b)   The Court can extend or abridge time wherever a time limit is fixed by the Rules but will only exercise this power where it is satisfied there are very good reasons for doing so. If an extension or abridgement of time is sought grounds in support of that application must be filed and verified by affidavit: Order 3 rule 5(1).

3   FEES

A fee of £50.00 is payable on lodging an application for leave to apply for Judicial Review. A further £70.00 is payable, if leave is granted, on entering an affidavit of service and notice of motion (total £120.00). Cheques should be made payable to H.M. Paymaster General. Personal cheques are not accepted unless supported by a bankers cheque guarantee card presented in the Fees Room at the time of lodging the application. Any application for a remission of this fee must be made in writing to the Supreme Court Accounts Office, Royal Courts of Justice in advance of lodging the application for leave.

4   FORM OF APPLICATION

Applications for leave to move for Judicial Review must be made in Form 86A and must be supported by an affidavit verifying the facts relied on: Order 5 rule 3(2). In addition to the original documents, the applicant must provide two copies, where the application is to be considered by a Divisional Court, and one copy in a civil case where the application is to be considered by a single Judge.

N.B. Where the documents in support of an application for leave exceed 10 pages, they must be paginated and indexed in a convenient bundle. In addition, a list must be provided of the pages essential for reading by the Court. Where only part of a page needs to be read, that part should be indicated, by side-lining or in some other way, but *not* by highlighting: Practice Direction [1994] 1 WLR 1551.

Where the applicant is represented by solicitors they must also provide a paginated, indexed bundle of the *relevant* legislative provisions and statutory instruments required for the proper consideration of the application. *An applicant who acts in person should comply with this requirement if possible:* Practice Direction, 6 December 1996.

Applications which do not comply with the requirements of both Practice Directions will *not* be accepted, even with undertakings to comply at a later date, save in exceptional circumstances such as urgency. In this context a matter will be regarded as urgent where a decision is required from the Court within 14 days of the lodging of the application. If the only reason given in support of urgency is the imminent expiry of the three month time limit for lodging an application, the papers will nonetheless be returned for compliance with the Practice Direction(s) and if necessary, the applicant must seek an extension of time and provide reasons for the delay in lodging the papers in proper form.

5   LEAVE TO MOVE

Ex parte applications for leave to move for Judicial Review will be considered in one of two ways on the papers or at an oral hearing in open court.

   (a)   Consideration on papers

Unless the applicant otherwise requests in his notice of application, the papers in the case will be placed before a Judge who will decide whether to grant leave to move without hearing any oral submissions. The purpose of this procedure is to ensure that applications may be dealt with speedily and without unnecessary expense. Applicants or their Solicitors will be informed of the Judge's decision on Form JRJ. If leave is refused, an applicant or his solicitor may renew the application in a criminal cause or matter to the Divisional Court and otherwise to a single Judge sitting in open Court by completing and returning Form 86B within 10 days of the notice of refusal being served upon him.

   (b)   Oral hearing in open court

If the notice of application contains such a request it may proceed directly to an oral hearing before a Judge in open Court. Where the Judge refuses leave an applicant or his solicitor may, in a criminal cause or matter *only*, renew his application for hearing by a Divisional Court by completing and lodging Form 86B within 10 days of the notice of refusal being served upon him. In a civil matter the Judge's decision is final so far as the High Court is concerned; an ex parte application for leave which has been refused by a Judge after a hearing may be renewed to the Court of Appeal Civil Division within 7 days. At an oral hearing an applicant may appear in person or be represented by Counsel. The name of Counsel must be given to the Crown Office as soon as it is known. The Crown Office will inform an applicant or his legal advisers, as the case may be, of the date fixed for any oral hearing: Order 53 rule 3(3)(4) and (5).

An oral hearing is allocated 20 minutes of court time. If counsel considers that 20 minutes is insufficient he must provide a written estimate of the time required and request a special fixture.

6   NOTICE OF MOTION

Where leave is granted the applicant or his solicitor must, within 14 days from the grant of leave, serve a notice of motion in Form 86 (together with a copy of the order granting leave) on all persons directly affected and enter a copy in the Crown Office together with an affidavit of service. The latter must give the names and addresses of, and the places and dates of service on, all persons who have been served with the notice of motion. If any person who ought to have been served has not been served the affidavit must state that fact and the reason for it: Order 53 rule 5(5) and (6).

7   RESPONDENTS

A party upon whom a notice of motion is served may, if he wishes, file an affidavit in reply (informing the Crown Office of his intention to do so as soon as practicable) and must file it as soon as practicable and in any event within 56 days after service, having given notice thereof to the applicant. He may be represented at the hearing and all parties who file affidavits will be informed of the date fixed for hearing.

8   HEARING OF MOTION

When an application is ready to be heard it will be entered in Part B of the Crown Office List; see the Practice Direction at [1987] 1 WLR 232 and [1987] 1 All ER 368, and the applicant or his solicitor informed. While the Crown Office will give as much notice as possible of the date fixed for hearing it cannot undertake to accommodate the wishes of applicants, respondents, their Solicitors or Counsel; in particular the occasional need to list cases at short notice may mean that parties are unable to be represented by the Counsel of their first choice. Applications in criminal causes or matters will be heard by a Divisional Court consisting of two or more Judges. Civil cases will generally be heard by a single Judge sitting in open Court but may be heard by a Divisional Court where the Court so directs: Order 53 rule 5(1) and (2).

9   EXPEDITION

Where leave to apply for Judicial Review has been granted, and an applicant believes that he has grounds for an expedited hearing of his application, he may apply by summons to the Master of the Crown Office to have his case entered in the Expedited List, Part D of the Crown Office List; see the Practice Direction referred to in paragraph 8 above.

10   COSTS

It is a general rule that the party which loses is ordered to pay the costs of the other side.

11   APPEALS

A.   Criminal matters

(i)   Substantive application

The Administration of Justice Act 1960 provides:

'S1(1)   Subject to the provisions of this section, an appeal shall lie to the House of Lords, at the instance of the defendant or the prosecutor—

(a)   from any decision of a Divisional Court of the Queens Bench Division in a criminal cause or matter:

(b)   ...

(2)   No appeal shall lie under this section except with the leave of the Court below or of the House of Lords; and such leave shall not be granted unless it is certified by the court below that a point of law of general public importance is involved in the decision and it appears to that court or to the House of Lords, as the case may be, that the point is one which ought to be considered by that House.'

(ii)   Where leave has been refused by the Divisional Court there is no right of appeal.

B.   Civil matters

(i)   In a substantive application in a civil matter appeal lies with leave of the Court to the Court of Appeal Civil Division.

(ii)

12   ADVICE

If in doubt about any procedural matter applicants, respondents or their advisers should direct their enquiries to the Crown Office, telephone number: 0171-936 6205.

The Crown Office
Royal Courts of Justice
Strand   12 January 1981
London WC2A 2LL   (revised 21 March 1997)

SUPREME COURT ACT 1981, SECTION 29
Orders of mandamus, prohibition and certiorari

29.—(1)   The High Court shall have jurisdiction to make orders of mandamus, prohibition and certiorari in those classes of cases in which it had power to do so immediately before the commencement of this Act.

(2)   Every such order shall be final, subject to any right of appeal therefrom.

(3)   In relation to the jurisdiction of the Crown Court, other than its jurisdiction in matters relating to trial on indictment, the High Court shall have all such jurisdiction to make orders of mandamus, prohibition or certiorari as the High Court possesses in relation to the jurisdiction of an inferior court.

(4)   The power of the High Court under any enactment to require justices of the peace or a judge or officer of a county court to do any act relating to the duties of their respective offices, or to require a magistrates' court to state a case for the opinion of the High Court, in any case where the High Court formerly had by virtue of any enactment jurisdiction to make a rule absolute, or an order, for any of those purposes, shall be exercisable by order of mandamus.

(5)   In any enactment—

(a)   references to a writ of mandamus, of prohibition or of certiorari shall be read as references to the corresponding order; and

(b)   references to the issue or award of any such writ shall be read as references to the making of the corresponding order.

SUPREME COURT ACT 1981, SECTION 31

Application for judicial review

31.—(1) An application to the High Court for one or more of the following forms of relief, namely—

    (a)   an order of mandamus, prohibition or certiorari;

    (b)   a declaration or injunction under subsection (2); or

    (c)   an injunction under section 30 restraining a person not entitled to do so from acting in an office to which that section applies,

shall be made in accordance with rules of court by a procedure to be known as an application for judicial review.

(2) A declaration may be made or an injunction granted under this subsection in any case where an application for judicial review, seeking that relief, has been made and the High Court considers that, having regard to—

    (a)   the nature of the matters in respect of which relief may be granted by orders of mandamus, prohibition or certiorari;

    (b)   the nature of the persons and bodies against whom relief may be granted by such orders; and

    (c)   all the circumstances of the case,

it would be just and convenient for the declaration to be made or the injunction to be granted, as the case may be.

(3) No application for judicial review shall be made unless the leave of the High Court has been obtained in accordance with rules of court: and the court shall not grant leave to make such an application unless it considers that the applicant has a sufficient interest in the matter to which the application relates.

(4) On an application for judicial review the High Court may award damages to the applicant if—

    (a)   he has joined with his application a claim for damages arising from any matter to which the application relates; and

    (b)   the court is satisfied that, if the claim had been made in an action begun by the applicant at the time of making his application, he would have been awarded damages.

(5) If, on an application for judicial review seeking an order of certiorari, the High Court quashes the decision to which the application relates, the High Court may remit the matter to the court, tribunal or authority concerned, with a direction to reconsider it and reach a decision in accordance with the findings of the High Court.

(6) Where the High Court considers that there has been undue delay in making an application for judicial review, the court may refuse to grant—

    (a)   leave for the making of the application; or

    (b)   any relief sought on the application,

if it considers that the granting of the relief sought would be likely to cause substantial hardship to, or substantially prejudice the rights of, any person or would be detrimental to good administration.

(7) Subsection (6) is without prejudice to any enactment or rule of court which has the effect of limiting the time within which an application for judicial review may be made.

SUPREME COURT ACT 1981, SECTION 43
Power of High Court to vary sentence on certiorari

43.—(1) Where a person who has been sentenced for an offence—

(a) by a magistrates' court; or

(b) by the Crown Court after being convicted of the offence by a magistrates' court and committed to the Crown Court for sentence; or

(c) by the Crown Court on appeal against conviction or sentence,

applies to the High Court in accordance with section 31 for an order of certiorari to remove the proceedings of the magistrates' court or the Crown Court into the High Court, then, if the High Court determines that the magistrates' court or the Crown Court had no power to pass the sentence, the High Court may, instead of quashing the conviction, amend it by substituting for the sentence passed any sentence which the magistrates' court or, in a case within paragraph (b), the Crown Court had power to impose.

(2) Any sentence passed by the High Court by virtue of this section in substitution for the sentence passed in the proceedings of the magistrates' court or the Crown Court shall, unless the High Court otherwise directs, begin to run from the time when it would have begun to run if passed in those proceedings; but in computing the term of the sentence, any time during which the offender was released on bail in pursuance of section 37(1)(d) of the Criminal Justice Act 1948 shall be disregarded.

(3) Subsections (1) and (2) shall, with the necessary modifications, apply in relation to any order of a magistrates' court or the Crown Court which is made on, but does not form part of, the conviction of an offender as they apply in relation to a conviction and sentence.

ORDER 53 OF THE RULES OF THE SUPREME COURT

ORDER 53

APPLICATIONS FOR JUDICIAL REVIEW

Cases appropriate for application for judicial review (O. 53, r. 1)

1.—(1)   An application for—

(a)   an order of mandamus, prohibition or certiorari, or

(b)   an injunction under section 30 of the Act restraining a person from acting in any office in which he is not entitled to act,

shall be made by way of an application for judicial review in accordance with the provisions of this Order.

(2)   An application for a declaration or an injunction (not being an injunction mentioned in paragraph (1)(b)) may be made by way of an application for judicial review, and on such an application the Court may grant the declaration or injunction claimed if it considers that, having regard to—

(a)   the nature of the matters in respect of which relief may be granted by way of an order of mandamus, prohibition or certiorari,

(b)   the nature of the persons and bodies against whom relief may be granted by way of such an order, and

(c)   all the circumstances of the case,

it would be just and convenient for the declaration or injunction to be granted on an application for judicial review.

Joinder of claims for relief (O. 53, r. 2)

2.   On an application for judicial review any relief mentioned in rule 1(1) or (2) may be claimed as an alternative or in addition to any other relief so mentioned if it arises out of or relates to or is connected with the same matter.

Grant of leave to apply for judicial review (O. 53, r. 3)

3.—(1)   No application for judicial review shall be made unless the leave of the Court has been obtained in accordance with this rule.

(2)   An application for leave must be made *ex parte* to a judge by filing in the Crown Office—

(a)   a notice in Form No. 86A containing a statement of

(i)   the name and description of the applicant,

(ii)   the relief sought and the grounds upon which it is sought,

(iii)   the name and address of the applicant's solicitors (if any) and

(iv)   the applicant's address for service; and

(b)   an affidavit which verifies the facts relied on.

(3)   The judge may determine the application without a hearing, unless a hearing is requested in the notice of application, and need not sit in open court; in any case, the Crown Office shall serve a copy of the judge's order on the applicant.

(4)   Where the application for leave is refused by the judge, or is granted on terms, the applicant may renew it by applying—

(a)   in any criminal cause or matter, to a Divisional Court of the Queen's Bench Division;

(b)   in any other case, to a single judge sitting in open court or, if the Court so directs, to a Divisional Court of the Queen's Bench Division:

Provided that no application for leave may be renewed in any non-criminal cause or matter in which the judge has refused leave under paragraph (3) after a hearing.

(5)   In order to renew his application for leave the applicant must, within 10 days of being served with notice of the judge's refusal, lodge in the Crown Office notice of his intention in Form No. 86B.

(6)   Without prejudice to its powers under Order 20, rule 8, the Court hearing an application for leave may allow the applicant's statement to be amended, whether by specifying different or additional grounds or relief or otherwise, on such terms, if any, as it thinks fit.

(7)   The Court shall not grant leave unless it considers that the applicant has a sufficient interest in the matter to which the application relates.

(8)   Where leave is sought to apply for an order of certiorari to remove for the purpose of its being quashed any judgment, order, conviction or other proceedings which is subject to appeal and a time is limited for the bringing of the appeal, the Court may adjourn the application for leave until the appeal is determined or the time for appealing has expired.

(9)   If the Court grants leave, it may impose such terms as to costs and as to giving security as it thinks fit.

(10)   Where leave to apply for judicial review is granted, then—

(a)   if the relief sought is an order of prohibition or certiorari and the Court so directs, the grant shall operate as a stay of the proceedings to which the application relates until the determination of the application or until the Court otherwise orders;

(b)   if any other relief is sought, the Court may at any time grant in the proceedings such interim relief as could be granted in an action begun by writ.

Delay in applying for relief (O. 53, r. 4)

4.—(1)   An application for leave to apply for judicial review shall be made promptly and in any event within three months from the date when grounds for the application first arose unless the Court considers that there is good reason for extending the period within which the application shall be made.

(2)   Where the relief sought is an order of certiorari in respect of any judgment, order, conviction or other proceeding, the date when grounds for the application first arose shall be taken to be the date of that judgment, order, conviction or proceeding.

(3)   The preceding paragraphs are without prejudice to any statutory provision which has the effect of limiting the time within which an application for judicial review may be made.

Mode of applying for judicial review (O. 53, r. 5)

5.—(1)   In any criminal cause or matter, where leave has been granted to make an application for judicial review, the application shall be made by originating motion to a Divisional Court of the Queen's Bench Division.

(2) In any other such cause or matter, the application shall be made by originating motion to a judge sitting in open court, unless the Court directs that it shall be made—

    (a) by originating summons to a judge in chambers; or

    (b) by originating motion to a Divisional Court of the Queen's Bench Division.

Any direction under sub-paragraph (a) shall be without prejudice to the judge's powers under Order 32, rule 13.

(3) The notice of motion or summons must be served on all persons directly affected and where it relates to any proceedings in or before a court and the object of the application is either to compel the court or an officer of the court to do any act in relation to the proceedings or to quash them or any order made therein, the notice or summons must also be served on the clerk or registrar of the court and, where any objection to the conduct of the judge is to be made, on the judge.

(4) Unless the Court granting leave has otherwise directed, there must be at least 10 days between the service of the notice of motion or summons and the hearing.

(5) A motion must be entered for hearing within 14 days after the grant of leave.

(6) An affidavit giving the names and addresses of, and the places and dates of service on, all persons who have been served with the notice of motion or summons must be filed before the motion or summons is entered for hearing and, if any person who ought to be served under this rule has not been served, the affidavit must state that fact and the reason for it; and the affidavit shall be before the Court on the hearing of the motion or summons.

(7) If on the hearing of the motion or summons the Court is of opinion that any person who ought, whether under this rule or otherwise, to have been served has not been served, the Court may adjourn the hearing on such terms (if any) as it may direct in order that the notice or summons may be served on that person.

Statements and affidavits (O. 53, r. 6)

6.—(1) Copies of the statement in support of an application for leave under rule 3 must be served with the notice of motion or summons and, subject to paragraph (2), no grounds shall be relied upon or any relief sought at the hearing except the grounds and relief set out in the statement.

(2) The Court may on the hearing of the motion or summons allow the applicant to amend his statement, whether by specifying different or additional grounds or relief or otherwise, on such terms, if any, as it thinks fit and may allow further affidavits to be used if they deal with new matters arising out of an affidavit of any other party to the application.

(3) Where the applicant intends to ask to be allowed to amend his statement or to use further affidavits, he shall give notice of his intention and of any proposed amendment to every other party.

(4) Any respondent who intends to use an affidavit at the hearing shall file it in the Crown Office as soon as practicable and in any event, unless the Court otherwise directs, within 56 days after service upon him of the documents required to be served by paragraph (1).

(5)   Each party to the application must supply to every other party on demand and on payment of the proper charges copies of every affidavit which he proposes to use at the hearing, including, in the case of the applicant, the affidavit in support of the application for leave under rule 3.

Claim for damages (O. 53, r. 7)

7.—(1)   On an application for judicial review the Court may, subject to paragraph (2), award damages to the applicant if—

(a)   he has included in the statement in support of his application for leave under rule 3 a claim for damages arising from any matter to which the application relates, and

(b)   the Court is satisfied that, if the claim had been made in an action begun by the applicant at the time of making his application, he could have been awarded damages.

(2)   Order 18, rule 12, shall apply to a statement relating to a claim for damages as it applies to a pleading.

Application for discovery, interrogatories, cross-examination etc. (O. 53, r. 8)

8.—(1)   Unless the Court otherwise directs, any interlocutory application in proceedings on an application for judicial review may be made to any judge or a master of the Queen's Bench Division, notwithstanding that the application for judicial review has been made by motion and is to be heard by a Divisional Court.

In this paragraph 'interlocutory application' includes an application for an order under Order 24 or 26 or Order 38, rule 2(3) or for an order dismissing the proceedings by consent of the parties.

(2)   In relation to an order made by a master pursuant to paragraph (1) Order 58, rule 1, shall, where the application for judicial review is to be heard by a Divisional Court, have effect as if a reference to that Court were substituted for the reference to a judge in chambers.

(3)   This rule is without prejudice to any statutory provision or rule of law restricting the making of an order against the Crown.

Hearing of application for judicial review (O. 53, r. 9)

9.—(1)   On the hearing of any motion or summons under rule 5, any person who desires to be heard in opposition to the motion or summons, and appears to the Court to be a proper person to be heard, shall be heard, notwithstanding that he has not been served with notice of the motion or the summons.

(2)   Where the relief sought is or includes an order of certiorari to remove any proceedings for the purpose of quashing them, the applicant may not question the validity of any order, warrant, commitment, conviction, inquisition or record unless before the hearing of the motion or summons he has lodged in the Crown Office a copy thereof verified by affidavit or accounts for his failure to do so to the satisfaction of the Court hearing the motion or summons.

(3)   Where an order for certiorari is made in any such case as is referred to in paragraph (2) the order shall, subject to paragraph (4), direct that the proceedings shall be quashed forthwith on their removal into the Queen's Bench Division.

(4)   Where the relief sought is an order of certiorari and the Court is satisfied that there are grounds for quashing the decision to which the application relates, the Court may, in addition to quashing it, remit the matter to the court, tribunal or authority concerned with a direction to reconsider it and reach a decision in accordance with the findings of the Court.

(5)   Where the relief sought is a declaration, an injunction or damages and the Court considers that it should not be granted on an application for judicial review but might have been granted if it had been sought in an action begun by writ by the applicant at the time of making his application, the Court may, instead of refusing the application, order the proceedings to continue as if they had been begun by writ; and Order 28, rule 8, shall apply as if, in the case of an application made by motion, it had been made by summons.

Saving for person acting in obedience to mandamus (O. 53, r. 10)

10.   No action or proceeding shall be begun or prosecuted against any person in respect of anything done in obedience to an order of mandamus.

Proceedings for disqualification of member of local authority (O. 53, r. 11)

11.—(1)   Proceedings under section 92 of the Local Government Act 1972 must be begun by originating motion to a Divisional Court of the Queen's Bench Division, and, unless otherwise directed, there must be at least 10 days between the service of the notice of motion and the hearing.

(2)   Without prejudice to Order 8, rule 3, the notice of motion must set out the name and description of the applicant, the relief sought and the grounds on which it is sought, and must be supported by affidavit verifying the facts relied on.

(3)   Copies of every supporting affidavit must be lodged in the Crown Office before the motion is entered for hearing and must be supplied to any other party on demand and on payment of the proper charges.

(4)   The provisions of rules 5, 6 and 9(1) as to the persons on whom the notice is to be served and as to the proceedings at the hearing shall apply, with the necessary modifications, to proceedings under the said section 92 as they apply to an application for judicial review.

Consolidation of applications (O. 53, r. 12)

12.   Where there is more than one application pending under section 30 of the Act, or section 92 of the Local Government Act 1972, against several persons in respect of the same office, and on the same grounds, the Court may order the applications to be consolidated.

Appeal from judge's order (O. 53, r. 13)

13.   No appeal shall lie from an order made under paragraph (3) of rule 3 on an application for leave which may be renewed under paragraph (4) of that rule.

Meaning of 'Court' (O. 53, r. 14)

14.   In relation to the hearing by a judge of an application for leave under rule 3 or of an application for judicial review, any reference in this Order to 'the Court' shall, unless the context otherwise requires, be construed as a reference to the judge.

11 Appeal by way of Case Stated

INTRODUCTION

Case stated is the procedure by which the High Court is able to review the decisions of inferior courts in respect of points of law. The remedy is available for decisions of magistrates' courts and Crown Courts sitting in their appellate capacity.

The procedure is available where there are no factual disputes, as the court is bound by the findings of fact stated by the magistrates' court or Crown Court, save where it is being said that there was no evidence on which a particular finding of fact could have been made.

There is clearly an overlap between case stated and judicial review, and it is often confusing to decide which remedy to pursue. Chapter 1 outlines some considerations, a primary one being the fact that an appeal to the Crown Court ceases on the stating of a case. In essence, however, case stated is not concerned with how a decision was reached but with its (legal) merits, unlike judicial review.

JURISDICTION

In magistrates' court proceedings, the authority for case stated arises from ss. 111–114, Magistrates' Courts Act 1980, and in Crown Court proceedings by virtue of s. 28, Supreme Court Act 1981. The above enactments are further supported by the Magistrates' Courts Rules 1981 and Crown Court Rules 1982. All relevant extracts are reproduced at the end of this chapter.

GROUNDS FOR CASE STATED

A person may ask the court to state a case for the consideration of the High Court in two instances, namely when:

- the decision made is wrong in law; or
- the court has acted in excess of its jurisdiction.

As will be seen later, the remedy is available to both prosecution and defence. A challenge could be made to a decision to convict or acquit, and even to allow a submission of no case to answer. It should be noted that not all errors of law are amenable to the case stated procedure. For example, a severe sentence which is outside normal discretion may well be classified as an error of law, but case stated should not be used. Similarly case stated is not an appropriate remedy where a breach of natural justice has occurred.

Examples

(1)   A police officer stops a car on the motorway. In the vehicle he finds a flick knife. The defendant at trial accepts that he was in possession of the knife, and also concedes that it is an offensive weapon. It is argued by the defendant, successfully, that he is not guilty due to the fact that the knife, being inside the car, was not in a public place.

This follows a real case (save that a dog was involved) where the Crown Prosecution Service appealed the justices' finding. The CPS argued that the justices had erred in law in holding a motor vehicle, which itself is on a public road, as not being a public place. The Divisional Court agreed with the prosecution (*Bates* v *DPP*, *The Times*, 8 March 1993).

(2)   The defendant appealed to the Crown Court against his conviction by justices. Two Crown Court hearings were ineffective, once due to lack of court time, secondly, due to prosecution difficulties. On the third hearing the defendant (appellant) failed to attend, but was represented by Counsel who had full instructions. An application to adjourn was refused and the Crown Court dismissed the appeal without hearing evidence.

It was held that since he was represented he was deemed to be present, and in the absence of an application to abandon the appeal the court should have proceeded to hear the evidence. The Crown Court accordingly had no power to dismiss the appeal, having not heard evidence. In essence the court had acted in excess of its jurisdiction (*Podmore* v *DPP* [1997] COD 80, DC, which is in fact a judicial review case).

WHO CAN APPEAL?

The following categories of persons may appeal:

- a party to the proceedings before the court; or
- any person aggrieved by a conviction, order, determination or other proceedings of the court.

However, in Crown Court appeals, section 28, Supreme Court Act 1981, limits the categories of persons to those who are a party to the proceedings. There would appear to be no good reason for this distinction.

The second category is wide enough to include any person affected by the judicial decision, but is likely to have little application in day-to-day criminal law.

AT WHAT STAGE CAN PROCEEDINGS BE APPEALED?

There must have been a final determination in the proceedings, whether that be conviction, sentence or acquittal. Case stated will not be available for example in committal proceedings (however, judicial review may well be).

PRACTICAL CONSIDERATIONS

By making an appeal by way of case stated, appeal remedies to the Crown Court cease. This rule has been interpreted strictly, and covers the situation where an application to state a case was made out of time and therefore was in fact invalid (*P & M Supplies (Essex) Ltd* v *Hackney* [1990] Crim LR 569).

It is, however, permissible to appeal by way of case stated against a conviction and then, if the appeal is lost, to appeal to the Crown Court against sentence (*Sivalingham* v *DPP* [1975] CLY 2037). Presumably the fact that a case has been stated will be good enough grounds for an appeal out of time or a stay of proceedings pending the determination of the case stated.

A stay of sentence pending the outcome of a case stated is not available, but see later for remedies in respect to bail and disqualifications.

PROCEDURE FOR STATING A CASE: MAGISTRATES' COURT

• A formal application is made to the court clerk, requesting the court clerk to state a case. The request should state the question of law or jurisdiction involved. The application must be in writing and signed by or on behalf of the applicant (s. 111, MCA 1980, r. 76(1), MCR 1981).

• The application must be made within 21 days after the day on which the decision of the magistrates' court was given (s. 111(2), MCA 1980). For the purposes of this rule, where the court has adjourned the trial of an information after conviction, the relevant day is the day on which the court sentences or otherwise deals with the offender (s. 111(3), MCA 1980). In *Liverpool City Council* v *Worthington, The Times*, 16 June 1998, it was held that if a decision on costs falls to be made, then that is capable of being the last day of the proceedings and accordingly the time limit runs from that date.

• Where one of the questions is whether there was evidence on which the magistrates' court could come to its decision, the particular finding of fact made by the magistrates' court which it is said cannot be supported by the evidence, must be specified in the application (r. 76(2), MCR 1981).

● At this stage the court can either state a case or refuse.

● The court can refuse to state a case if the justices are of the opinion that the application is frivolous. In such cases the applicant is entitled to a certificate to that effect. Where the Attorney General makes the application to state a case the justices may not refuse (s. 111(5), MCA 1980). The only remedy open to an applicant in these circumstances is to apply to the High Court for an order of mandamus, requiring the justices to state a case. Such an application is made by way of judicial review (s. 111(6), MCA 1980). In *Knightsbridge Crown Court, ex parte Foot, The Times*, 18 February 1998, it was said *obiter* that it may well be better just to judicially review the original decision instead — particularly where the facts are not in dispute. This applies equally to Crown Court refusals to state a case.

● If the justices agree to state a case (or the High Court orders one to be stated), the court must prepare a draft case and serve it on both the applicant and respondent (or their solicitors) within 21 days of the application having been made.

● The draft case must contain the matters stated within r. 81, MCR 1981, namely: the facts found by the court and the question or questions of law or jurisdiction on which the opinion of the High Court is sought. Further, where it is said that there was no evidence on which a finding could have been reached, the particular finding must be specified. The case must not contain a statement of evidence unless there is a question which asks whether there is evidence on which a particular finding could have been made.

● Within 21 days of receiving the draft, each party may make representations thereon (r. 77(2), MCR 1981), such representations must be made in writing, and signed by or on behalf of the person making them.

● Rule 79, MCR 1981 makes provision for the extension of time limits.

● Once the period for making representations is up, the court has 21 days thereafter to state a case, in its final form. It is a matter for the justices whether they make any adjustments as a result of the representations made.

● It is in the applicant's interest to try to influence the final case which is stated. To that end it is advised that the fullest arguments are set out at the outset. In many cases it would appear that the justices' clerk, who will be responsible for drafting the case, may well have been heavily influenced by the initial request to draft a case.

● Once the applicant is in receipt of the case, it must be lodged at the Crown Office within 10 days (RSC Ord. 56, r. 1(4)) and notice of entry of appeal served upon the respondent within four days thereafter (RSC Ord. 56, r. 4).

PROCEDURE FOR STATING A CASE: CROWN COURT

Rule 26, Crown Court Rules 1982, provides the detail:

● An application must be made in writing to the appropriate officer of the Crown Court, within 21 days of the date of the decision in respect of which the application is made (CCR, r. 26(1)).

- The court can require the appellant to enter into a recognizance to prosecute the appeal (this also applies in the case stating of magistrates' court matters).
- The application must state the ground on which the decision of the Crown Court is questioned (CCR, r. 26(2)).
- It is a matter for the judge as to whether a case is stated. Notification must be given to the parties in writing.
- If the judge refuses to state a case on the grounds that the application is frivolous, a certificate must be issued to that effect if required by the applicant (CCR, r. 26(6)). The remedy available here is judicial review, as described above.
- If the judge allows a case to be stated, the appellant must draft a case and send it to the judge and all other parties within 21 days of receiving notice of the judge's decision (CCR, r. 26(8)).
- Procedurally an applicant will often draft a case and send it with the initial request to save time. It is also an opportunity to convince a judge of the merits before he decides.
- Within 21 days of the draft, each party must do one of the following, namely, (a) indicate in writing that the draft is acceptable, (b) draft an alternative case, or (c) signify that they do not wish to take part in the proceedings (CCR, r. 26(9)).
- The judge will then consider the draft and any representations. The judge must then state and sign a case within 14 days.
- Time limits can be extended. However, in *Director of Public Prosecutions* v *Coleman, The Times*, 13 December 1997, DC, the court stated, in relation to prosecution extensions, that:

> An extension of time should be granted to the prosecution against an acquitted defendant only in exceptional circumstances and never without permitting the acquitted defendant the opportunity to make representations. The defendant should be notified of the application to extend time and the terms of the application should be disclosed to him and he should be told of his right to make representations. The prosecution should provide cogent reasons in an application to extend time and they should be considered against the background that an acquitted defendant had some expectation that, subject to Rule 26(1), the case was at an end.

- CCR, r. 26(13) states the contents of the case. However, it is couched in similar terms to the proforma Form 155 used in the magistrates' court.
- Three copies of the case must be lodged at the Crown Office within 10 days. A copy of the decision appealed against (the court memorandum) must be enclosed, including the magistrates' court decision.

AMENDMENTS TO THE CASE

The High Court may remit a case to the court for amendment. In respect of a case stated originating from a magistrates' court, the High Court may choose to amend the case itself as opposed to sending it back.

Any party can apply for the case to be amended, the application being made by way of notice of motion, accompanied by an affidavit.

This is a powerful remedy where a case is stated which is not agreed by the parties.

THE HEARING

The proceedings are by way of legal argument. It matters not whether the respondent appears, it is still for the applicant to show that the decision is wrong. Affidavits are not used, nor do justices generally appear, although if counsel (or a solicitor/advocate) has been instructed on their behalf they address the court (with leave).

It is not open to challenge the justices' findings of fact (the issues being purely legal), save where it is being argued that there was no evidence on which the finding could have made.

POWERS

Section 28A of the Supreme Court Act 1981 provides the remedies. The court may:

● reverse, affirm or amend the determination in respect of which the case has been stated (note, however, that this does not allow the court to reduce a sentence, for example — it must remit for that to be done); or
● remit the decision to the justices with the opinion of the court; and
● make such other order in relation to the matter (including costs) as it thinks fit.

The powers are far-reaching, enabling the court to acquit an appellant, or direct the court below to convict the appellant. The court may proceed to sentence itself (following the overturning of an acquittal). The court can order a rehearing (*Griffith v Jenkins* [1992] 2 AC 76).

PRACTICE DIRECTIONS AND PROCEDURAL GUIDANCE

● An applicant can withdraw an appeal at any time without leave of the court (*Collett* v *Bromsgrove DC* [1996] TLR 430).
● *Practice Direction (Evidence: Documents)* [1983] 1 WLR 922, deals with the marking, numbering and binding of documents and must be followed to the letter.
● *Practice Direction (Crown Office List: Uncontested Proceedings)* [1997] 2 All ER 801, details the procedure for submitting consent orders.
● *Practice Direction* [1972] 1 All ER 286, emphasises that evidence should not be included in the body of the case, unless it is being contended that there was no evidence on which the finding could have been made. Further, it should be unnecessary in instances where an appellant has been competently represented to delay the stating of the case in order to obtain the clerk's notes of evidence.
● *Practice Direction (Case Stated by Crown Courts)* (1978) 68 Cr App R 119, states that the form of case stated from the Crown Court should be the same as that for the magistrates' court, with necessary amendments only.

● The magistrates' court, Crown Court or High Court can suspend a disqualification pending an appeal by way of case stated (Road Traffic Offenders Act 1988, ss. 39–43).

● Bail may be granted pending an appeal. The magistrates' jurisdiction in this respect derives from s. 113, MCA 1980. In the magistrates' court there will be a condition of bail that the appellant must return to the court within 10 days of the High Court determination, unless the justices' decision is reversed.

● Legal aid is available and application must be made to the Legal Aid Board, in the normal manner.

MAGISTRATES' COURTS ACT 1980, SECTIONS 111–114 AND 148

Case Stated

Statement of Case by Magistrates' Court

111.—(1)   Any person who was a party to any proceeding before a magistrates' court or is aggrieved by the conviction, order, determination or other proceeding of the court may question the proceeding on the ground that it is wrong in law or is in excess of jurisdiction by applying to the justices composing the court to state a case for the opinion of the High Court on the question of law or jurisdiction involved; but a person shall not make an application under this section in respect of a decision against which he has a right of appeal to the High Court or which by virtue of any enactment passed after 31 December 1879 is final.

(2)   An application under subsection (1) above shall be made within 21 days after the day on which the decision of the magistrates' court was given.

(3)   For the purpose of subsection (2) above, the day on which the decision of the magistrates' court is given shall, where the court has adjourned the trial of an information after conviction, be the day on which the court sentences or otherwise deals with the offender.

(4)   On the making of an application under this section in respect of a decision any right of the applicant to appeal against the decision to the Crown Court shall cease.

(5)   If the justices are of opinion that an application under this section is frivolous, they may refuse to state a case, and, if the applicant so requires, shall give him a certificate stating that the application has been refused; but the justices shall not refuse to state a case if the application is made by or under the direction of the Attorney General.

(6)   Where justices refuse to state a case, the High Court may, on the application of the person who applied for the case to be stated, make an order of mandamus requiring the justices to state a case.

Effect of Decision of High Court on Case Stated by Magistrates' Court

112.   Any conviction, order, determination or other proceeding of a magistrates' court varied by the High Court on an appeal by case stated, and any judgment or order of the High Court on such an appeal, may be enforced as if it were a decision of the magistrates' court from which the appeal was brought.

Supplemental Provisions as to Appeal and Case Stated

Bail on Appeal or Case Stated

113.—(1)   Where a person has given notice of appeal to the Crown Court against the decision of a magistrates' court or has applied to a magistrates' court to state a case for the opinion of the High Court, then, if he is in custody, the magistrates' court may grant him bail.

(2)   If a person is granted bail under subsection (1) above, the time and place at which he is to appear (except in the event of the determination in respect of which the case is stated being reversed by the High Court) shall be—

(a)   if he has given notice of appeal, the Crown Court at the time appointed for the hearing of the appeal;

(b)   if he has applied for the statement of a case, the magistrates' court at such time within 10 days after the judgment of the High Court has been given as may be specified by the magistrates' court;

and any recognizance that may be taken from him or from any surety for him shall be conditioned accordingly.

(3)   Subsection (1) above shall not apply where the accused has been committed to the Crown Court for sentence under section 37 or 38 above.

(4)   Section 37(6) of the Criminal Justice Act 1948 (which relates to the currency of a sentence while a person is released on bail by the High Court) shall apply to a person released on bail by a magistrates' court under this section pending the hearing of a case stated as it applies to a person released on bail by the High Court under section 22 of the Criminal Justice Act 1967.

Recognizances and Fees on Case Stated

114.   Justices to whom application has been made to state a case for the opinion of the High Court on any proceeding of a magistrates' court shall not be required to state the case until the applicant has entered into a recognizance, with or without sureties, before the magistrates' court, conditioned to prosecute the appeal without delay and to submit to the judgment of the High Court and pay such costs as that Court may award; and (except in any criminal matter) the clerk of a magistrates' court shall not be required to deliver the case to the applicant until the applicant has paid him the fees payable for the case and for the recognizances.

. . .

148.—(1)   In this Act the expression 'magistrates' court' means any justice or justices of the peace acting under any enactment or by virtue of his or their commission or under the common law.

MAGISTRATES' COURTS RULES 1981 (S.I. 1981 No. 552 AS AMENDED) RR. 76–81

Case Stated

Application to state case

76.—(1)   An application under section 111(1) of the Act of 1980 shall be made in writing and signed by or on behalf of the applicant and shall identify the question or questions of law or jurisdiction on which the opinion of the High Court is sought.

(2)   Where one of the questions on which the opinion of the High Court is sought is whether there was evidence on which the magistrates' court could come to its decision, the particular finding of fact made by the magistrates' court which it is claimed cannot be supported by the evidence before the magistrates' court shall be specified in such application.

(3)   Any such application shall be sent to the clerk of the magistrates' court whose decision is questioned.

Consideration of draft case

77.—(1)   Within 21 days after receipt of an application made in accordance with rule 76, the clerk of the magistrates' court whose decision is questioned shall, unless the justices refuse to state a case under section 111(5) of the Act of 1980, send a draft case in which are stated the matters required under rule 81 to the applicant or his solicitor and shall send a copy thereof to the respondent or his solicitor.

(2)   Within 21 days after receipt of the draft case under paragraph (1), each party may make representations thereon. Any such representations shall be in writing and signed by or on behalf of the party making them and shall be sent to the clerk.

(3)   Where the justices refuse to state a case under section 111(5) of the Act and they are required by the High Court by order of mandamus under section 111(6) to do so, this rule shall apply as if in paragraph (1)—

(a)   for the words 'receipt of an application made in accordance with rule 76' there were substituted the words 'the date on which an order of mandamus under section 111(6) of the Act of 1980 is made'; and

(b)   the words 'unless the justices refuse to state a case under section 111(5) of the Act of 1980' were omitted.

Preparation and submission of final case

78.—(1)   Within 21 days after the latest day on which representations may be made under rule 77, the justices whose decision is questioned shall make such adjustments, if any, to the draft case prepared for the purposes of that rule as they think fit, after considering any such representations, and shall state and sign the case.

(2)   A case may be stated on behalf of the justices whose decision is questioned by any 2 or more of them and may, if the justices so direct, be signed on their behalf by their clerk.

(3)   Forthwith after the case has been stated and signed the clerk of the court shall send it to the applicant or his solicitor, together with any statement required by rule 79.

Extension of time limits
79.—(1)   If the clerk of a magistrates' court is unable to send to the applicant a draft case under paragraph (1) of rule 77 within the time required by that paragraph, he shall do so as soon as practicable thereafter and the provisions of that rule shall apply accordingly; but in that event the clerk shall attach to the draft case, and to the final case when it is sent to the applicant or his solicitor under rule 78(3), a statement of the delay and the reasons therefor.

(2)   If the clerk of a magistrates' court receives an application in writing from or on behalf of the applicant or the respondent for an extension of the time within which representations on the draft case may be made under paragraph (2) of rule 77, together with reasons in writing therefor, he may by notice in writing sent to the applicant or respondent as the case may be extend the time and the provisions of that paragraph and of rule 78 shall apply accordingly; but in that event the clerk shall attach to the final case, when it is sent to the applicant or his solicitor under rule 78(3), a statement of the extension and the reasons therefor.

(3)   If the justices are unable to state a case within the time required by paragraph (1) of rule 78, they shall do so as soon as practicable thereafter and the provisions of that rule shall apply accordingly; but in that event the clerk shall attach to the final case, when it is sent to the applicant or his solicitor under rule 78(3), a statement of the delay and the reasons therefor.

Service of documents
80.   Any document required by rules 76 to 79 to be sent to any person shall either be delivered to him or be sent by post in a registered letter or by recorded delivery service and, if sent by post to an applicant or respondent, shall be addressed to him at his last known or usual place of abode.

Content of case
81.—(1)   A case stated by the magistrates' court shall state the facts found by the court and the question or questions of law or jurisdiction on which the opinion of the High Court is sought.

(2)   Where one of the questions on which the opinion of the High Court is sought is whether there was evidence on which the magistrates' court could come to its decision, the particular finding of fact which it is claimed cannot be supported by the evidence before the magistrates' court shall be specified in the case.

(3)   Unless one of the questions on which the opinion of the High Court is sought is whether there was evidence on which the magistrates' court could come to its decision, the case shall not contain a statement of evidence.

Supreme Court Act 1981, s. 28

Appeals from Crown Court and inferior courts

28.—(1)   Subject to subsection (2), any order, judgment or other decision of the Crown Court may be questioned by any party to the proceedings, on the ground that it is wrong in law or is in excess of jurisdiction, by applying to the Crown Court to have a case stated by that court for the opinion of the High Court.

(2)   Subsection (1) shall not apply to—

(a)   a judgment or other decision of the Crown Court relating to trial on indictment; or

(b)   any decision of that court under the Betting, Gaming and Lotteries Act 1963, the Licensing Act 1964, the Gaming Act 1986 or the Local Government (Miscellaneous) Provisions Act 1982 which, by any provision of any of those Acts, is to be final.

(3)   Subject to the provisions of this Act and to rules of court, the High Court shall, in accordance with section 19(2), have jurisdiction to hear and determine—

(a)   any application, or any appeal (whether by way of case stated or otherwise), which it has power to hear and determine under or by virtue of this or any other Act; and

(b)   all such other appeals as it had jurisdiction to hear and determine immediately before the commencement of this Act.

ORDER 56, RR. 1 AND 4 OF THE RULES OF THE SUPREME COURT

ORDER 56

Appeals etc to High Court by Case Stated: General

Appeals from the Crown Court by Case Stated (O. 56, r. 1)

1.—(1) Except where they relate to affiliation proceedings or to care proceedings under the Children and Young Persons Act 1969, all appeals from the Crown Court by case stated shall be heard and determined-

(a) in any criminal cause or matter, by a Divisional Court of the Queen's Bench Division;

(b) in any other cause or matter, by a single judge sitting in court, or if the Court so directs, by a Divisional Court of the Queen's Bench Division.

(2) *[Revoked by R.S.C. (Amendment No. 5) 1971 (S.I. 1971 No. 1955).]*

(3) An appeal from the Crown Court by case stated shall not be entered for hearing unless and until the case and a copy of the judgment, order or decision in respect of which the case has been stated and, if that judgment, order or decision was given or made on an appeal to the Crown Court, a copy of the judgment, order or decision appealed from, have been lodged in the Crown Office.

(4) No such appeal shall be entered after the expiration of 10 days from the receipt by the appellant of the case unless the delay is accounted for to the satisfaction of the Divisional Court.

Notice of intention to apply for an extension of time for entry of the appeal must be served on the respondent at least 2 clear days before the day named in the notice for the hearing of the application.

(5) Where any such appeal has not been entered by reason of a default in complying with the provisions of this rule, the Crown Court may proceed as if no case had been stated.

Notice of Entry of Appeal (O. 56, r. 4)

4. Within 4 days after an appeal from the Crown Court by case stated is entered for hearing, the appellant must serve notice of the entry of the appeal on the respondent.

Crown Court Rules 1982, r. 26

Application to Crown Court to state case

26.—(1)   An application under section 28 of the Supreme Court Act 1981 to the Crown Court to state a case for the opinion of the High Court shall be made in writing to the appropriate officer of the Crown Court within 21 days after the date of the decision in respect of which the application is made.

(2)   The application shall state the ground on which the decision of the Crown Court is questioned.

(3)   After making the application, the applicant shall forthwith send a copy of it to the parties to the proceedings in the Crown Court.

(4)   On receipt of the application, the appropriate officer of the Crown Court shall forthwith send it to the judge who presided at the proceedings in which the decision was made.

(5)   On receipt of the application, the judge shall inform the appropriate officer of the Crown Court as to whether or not he has decided to state a case and that officer shall give notice in writing to the applicant of the judge's decision.

(6)   If the judge considers that the application is frivolous, he may refuse to state a case and shall in that case, if the applicant so requires, cause a certificate stating the reasons for the refusal to be given to him.

(7)   If the judge decides to state a case, the procedure to be followed shall, unless the judge in a particular case otherwise directs, be the procedure set out in paragraphs (8) to (12).

(8)   The applicant shall, within 21 days of receiving the notice referred to in paragraph (5), draft a case and send a copy of it to the appropriate officer of the Crown Court and to the parties to the proceedings in the Crown Court.

(9)   Each party to the proceedings in the Crown Court shall, within 21 days of receiving a copy of the draft case under paragraph (8), either—

(a)   give notice in writing to the applicant and the appropriate officer of the Crown Court that he does not intend to take part in the proceedings before the High Court; or

(b)   indicate in writing the copy of the draft case that he agrees with it and send the copy to the appropriate officer of the Crown Court; or

(c)   draft an alternative case and send it, together with the copy of the applicant's case, to the appropriate officer of the Crown Court.

(10)   The judge shall consider the applicant's draft case and any alternative draft case sent to the appropriate officer of the Crown Court under paragraph (9)(c).

(11)   If the Crown Court so orders, the applicant shall, before the case is stated and delivered to him, enter before an officer of the Crown Court into a recognizance, with or without sureties and in such sum as the Crown Court considers proper, having regard to the means of the applicant, conditioned to prosecute the appeal without delay.

(12)   The judge shall state and sign a case within 14 days after either—

(a)   the receipt of all the documents required to be sent to the appropriate officer of the Crown Court under paragraph (9); or

(b)   the expiration of the period of 21 days referred to in that paragraph, whichever is the sooner.

(13)   A case stated by the Crown Court shall state the facts found by the Crown Court, the submissions of the parties (including any authorities relied on by the parties during the course of those submissions), the decision of the Crown Court in respect of which the application is made and the question on which the opinion of the High Court is sought.

(14)   Any time limit referred to in this Rule may be extended either before or after it expires by the Crown Court.

(15)   If the judge decides not to state a case but the stating of a case is subsequently required by the High Court by order of mandamus, paragraphs (7) to (14) shall apply to the stating of the case save that—

(a)   in paragraph (7) the words 'If the judge decides to state a case' shall be omitted; and

(b)   in paragraph (8) for the words 'receiving the notice referred to in paragraph (5)' there shall be substituted the words 'the day on which the order of mandamus was made'.

APPLICATION TO JUSTICES TO STATE A CASE

To .... and .... two of Her Majesty's Justices of the Peace for the
.................., and to the Clerk of the Magistrates' Court sitting at ....

WHEREAS an information [or complaint] wherein I the undersigned was informant
[or prosecutor or complainant] [or wherein AB of .... was informant or
prosecutor or complainant] and CD was defendant [or respondent] [or I the
undersigned was defendant or respondent] was heard before and determined by the
.... Magistrates' Court on ....
NOW I, the undersigned, being aggrieved and dissatisfied with your determination
upon the hearing of the above information [or complaint] as being wrong in law or
in excess of jurisdiction hereby apply, pursuant to the Magistrates' Courts Act 1980,
section 111, to you to state and sign a case for the opinion of the High Court of Justice
on the following question, namely:
[state question of law]

....

Signed.

FORM 155 OF MAGISTRATES' COURTS (FORMS) RULES 1981 (S.I. 1981 No. 553)

FORM 155

Case Stated (M.C. Act 1980, s. 111; M.C. Rules 1981, rr. 78, 81)

In the High Court of Justice
Queen's Bench Division
Between A.B.,   Appellant
                                        and
         C.D.,   Respondent.

Case stated by Justices for the [county of   , acting in and for
   the Petty Sessional Division of   ], in respect of their
   adjudication as a Magistrates' Court sitting at

CASE

1. On the   day of   , 19   , an information [*or* complaint] was pre-
    ferred by the appellant [*or* respondent] against the respondent [*or* appellant] that
    he/she (*state shortly particulars of information or complaint and refer to any
    relevant statutes*).
2. We heard that said information [*or* complaint] on the
    day of   , 19   , and found the following facts:— (*set out in separate
    lettered paragraphs*).
[The following is a short statement of the evidence:—(*set out so as to show relevant
evidence given by each witness*).]
3. It was contended by the appellant that
4. It was contended by the respondent that
5. We were referred to the following cases
6. We were of opinion that (*state grounds of decision*) and accordingly (*state
    decision including any sentence or order*).

QUESTION

7. The question for the opinion of the High Court is

Dated   the day of   , 19
                                    E.F.,
                                    G.H.,

                                    Justices of the Peace for the [county]
                                    aforesaid [on behalf of all the Justices
                                    adjudicating].

APPLICATION TO CROWN COURT TO STATE CASE

BETWEEN:

AB   *Appellants*

and

CD   *Respondents*

WHEREAS the above-named [Appellants/Respondents] are aggrieved and dissatisfied with the determination of His Honour Judge .... [and Justices] given on .... upon the hearing of [*specify*] as being wrong in law or in excess of jurisdiction.

Application is hereby made pursuant to the Supreme Court Act 1981, section 28(1), that a case may be stated, as attached hereto, for the opinion of the High Court.

DATED ....

....
(Signed)

**NOTICE OF ENTRY OF
CASE STATED APPEAL**

In the High Court of Justice   CO/
Queen's Bench Division
[Divisional Court]

Between:

AB   *Appellants*

and

CD   *Respondents*

TAKE NOTICE that the above-named Appellants being the defendants to an information [or complaint] preferred by the Respondents and heard before and determined by [specify] on ...., being dissatisfied with the determination of the said justices as being wrong in law or in excess of jurisdiction, applied to the said justices pursuant to the Magistrates' Courts Act 1980, section 111, to state and sign a case for the opinion of [the Divisional Court of] the Queen's Bench Division of the High Court of Justice.

AND FURTHER TAKE NOTICE that in pursuance thereof the said justices have stated and signed a case copy of which is annexed hereto.

AND FURTHER TAKE NOTICE that this case has been entered for hearing before [the Divisional Court of] the Queen's Bench Division of the High Court of Justice at the Royal Courts of Justice, Strand, London WC2A 2LL [on .... or so soon thereafter as Counsel can be heard on behalf of the Appellants].

DATED: ....

....
(Signed)

To: ....

12   Appeals to the House of Lords

INTRODUCTION

An aggrieved defendant, who has failed to have a conviction overturned in the Crown Court, has no further avenue of appeal, save by way of case stated or judicial review.

The appellate jurisdiction of the House of Lords is, however, exercised over the High Court. Accordingly, a party aggrieved at the outcome of an appeal by way of case stated, or an application for judicial review, may have a further remedy open.

AVAILABILITY OF APPEAL

Administration of Justice Act 1960

1(1)   Subject to the provisions of this section, an appeal shall lie to the House of Lords, at the instance of the defendant or prosecutor—

(a)   from any decision of a Divisional Court of the Queen's Bench Division in a criminal cause or matter.

(2)   No appeal shall lie under this section except with the leave of the court below or of the House of Lords; and such leave shall not be granted unless it is certified by the court below that a point of law of general public importance is involved in the decision and it appears to that court or to the House of Lords, as the case may be, that the point is one which ought to be considered by that House.

Two Stage Process

The Divisional Court must first certify a point of law of general public importance. If the court refuses so to certify, that is the end of the matter, the House of Lords having no power to consider the matter.

After certification, an applicant must convince either the Divisional Court or the House of Lords that the point is one that ought to be considered by the House. As a matter of practice an applicant should always first ask the lower court for leave.

It has become almost standard practice for a lower court to refuse leave after certifying a point of general public importance, the matter being left to the House of Lords. The reason for this is simply that the view of the judiciary is that the Lords of Appeal in Ordinary should decide which matters are worthy of appeal.

One point of note is that the House of Lords will not consider the merits of any sentence, where the sentence passed was within the discretion of the Court. Accordingly, if judicial review or case stated is refused on a point relating to sentence, that is the end of the matter (*Ashdown* (1974) 58 Cr App R 339, CA).

MAKING THE APPLICATION

Reproduced at the end of the chapter are the Practice Directions applicable to criminal appeals, which detail the procedures to be followed. The main rules are:

● The application to the lower court must be made within 14 days of the decision of the lower court.
● If leave is refused (but a point is certified), an application can be made to the House of Lords. Such application is to be made within 14 days of the refusal.
● The defendant may apply for an extension of the 14 day time limit. The prosecutor may not.
● The House of Lords has no power to grant legal aid. Generally applications should still be made to the court in the absence of legal aid, but if not, should be made no later than 14 days after the final determination of the legal aid application. The petition will need to include a formal application to extend the time limit for appeal.
● If leave is granted by the court below (and this will be rare), the petition must be lodged within three months of the date of the order appealed from.
● The House of Lords does not grant bail: an application must be made to the court below.

POWER TO SUSPEND DISQUALIFICATION

ROAD TRAFFIC OFFENDERS ACT 1988, s. 40

(3)   Where a person ordered to be disqualified has appealed or applied for leave to appeal to the House of Lords—

(a)   under section 1 of the Administration of Justice Act 1960 from any decision of a Divisional Court of the Queen's Bench Division which is material to his conviction or sentence, or

(b)   [not relevant]

the Divisional Court or, as the case may require, the Court of Appeal may, if it thinks fit, suspend the disqualification.

(4)   [not relevant]

(5)   [not relevant]

(6)   Any power of a court under the preceding provisions of this section to suspend the disqualification of any person is a power to do so on such terms as the court thinks fit.

(7)   Where, by virtue of this section, a court suspends the disqualification of any person, it must send notice of the suspension to the Secretary of State.

(8)   The notice must be sent in such manner and to such address and must contain such particulars as the Secretary of State may determine.

CONCLUSION

Clearly, the number of appeals to the House of Lords arising from a conviction in the magistrates' court, will be small. However, it is critical to consider all appeal avenues if justice is to be done to a particular defendant's case.

As far as the criminal justice system in England and Wales is concerned, the House of Lords is the final avenue of appeal.

It is debatable whether European remedies truly fall into the ambit of a book on appeal, as they deal with the applicability of European legal principles to English law, rather than the merits of any particular decision or the way in which it was reached. European law does, however, need to be considered and applied along the way, and that is a complete area of law in itself, outside the scope of this work.

An area of law which does in many instances relate to the decision making process and the decisions themselves, is the European Convention on Human Rights. A party denied legal aid for example may fail to have that decision appealed or reviewed successfully in an English court, and may seek redress in Europe. Again, such rights are outside the scope of this text, save to remind practitioners of their availability. The situation at the present time is further confused by the Human Rights Act 1998, which received the Royal Assent on 9 November 1998 but only a very small part of which is in force. This Act enshrines the European Convention principles in English law and allows the courts to declare English law inconsistent with Convention principles.

For an excellent summary of the Convention and some of the challenges made to date, see *Archbold (1999), Chapter 16.*

HOUSE OF LORDS
PRACTICE DIRECTIONS APPLICABLE TO CRIMINAL APPEALS
I.   PETITIONS FOR LEAVE TO APPEAL

1.   LEAVE TO APPEAL

England, Wales and Northern Ireland
1.1   An appeal lies to the House of Lords only with the leave of the court below or of the House. In criminal causes, an appeal lies to the House of Lords at the instance of the defendant or prosecutor:

(a)   from any decision of the Court of Appeal (Criminal Division) on an appeal to that court;

(b)   from any decision of a Divisional Court of the Queen's Bench Division in a criminal cause or matter;

(c)   from any decision of the Courts-Martial Appeal Court on an appeal to that court;

(d)   from any decision of the Court of Appeal in Northern Ireland on an appeal to that court by a person convicted on indictment;

(e)   from any decision of the Court of Appeal in Northern Ireland in a criminal cause or matter on a case stated by a county court or magistrates' court;

(f)   from any decision of the High Court of Justice in Northern Ireland in a criminal cause or matter.

In cases involving criminal contempt of court, an appeal lies to the House of Lords at the instance of the defendant and, in respect of an application for committal or attachment, at the instance of the applicant from any decision of the Court of Appeal (Criminal Division), the Courts-Martial Appeal Court or a Divisional Court of the Queen's Bench Division.

Scotland
1.2   No appeal lies to the House of Lords from the High Court of Justiciary.

2.   CERTIFICATE OF POINT OF LAW

2.1   Leave to appeal in a criminal cause or matter will only be granted if it is certified by the court below that a point of law of general public importance is involved in the decision of that court, and if it appears to that court or to the House that the point is one that ought to be considered by the House.
2.2   A certificate is not required for an appeal from a decision of a Divisional Court of the Queen's Bench Division or of the High Court in Northern Ireland on a criminal application for habeas corpus.
2.3   A certificate is not required in contempt of court cases where the decision of the court below was not a decision on appeal.

3. TIME LIMITS

3.1   Application for leave to appeal to the House of Lords must first be made to the court below. Such application must be made within fourteen days of the date of the decision of that court. This requirement also applies to contempt of court and habeas corpus cases whether a certificate is granted or not.

3.2   Applications to the House of Lords for leave to appeal must be made within fourteen days of the refusal of such leave by the court below. This date is not necessarily that on which the point of law was certified. Where the time prescribed expires on a Saturday, Sunday, Bank Holiday or other day on which the Judicial Office is closed, the application will be accepted if received on the next ensuing day on which the Judicial Office is open.

Application for extension of time

3.3   The House of Lords or the court below may, on application made at any time by the defendant but not the prosecutor, extend the time within which application for leave to appeal to the House may be made to the House, or to that court. Such an application to the House should be made on the petition for leave itself, and should set out briefly the reasons why the petition is outside the statutory fourteen-day period. These reasons should not normally exceed a paragraph in length. For form of petition, see Appendix B.

Legal Aid

3.4   Where, in an application for leave to appeal from an order of a Divisional Court of the Queen's Bench Division, an application for legal aid has been made to the Legal Aid Board (or, in Northern Ireland, to the Legal Aid Committee) and such an application has not been determined within the statutory fourteen-day period (see Direction 3.1), an application should be made, within fourteen days of the final determination of the legal aid application, for an extension of the time within which the petition for leave may be lodged (see Direction 3.3).

4. LODGMENT OF PETITION

4.1   Applications to the House of Lords for leave to appeal are made by petition. Such a petition should set out briefly the facts and points of law and conclude with summarised reasons why leave to appeal should be granted. For form of petition, see Appendix A.

4.2   No petition for leave to appeal may be lodged in the Judicial Office for presentation to the House unless the certificate required by statute (see Direction 2) has been granted by the court below.

4.3   A petition for leave to appeal must be signed by the petitioner or his agents.

Title

4.4   Petitions for leave to appeal to the House of Lords carry the same title as the cause in the court below, but the parties are described as petitioners and respondents.

'Regina' is used in the title. In any petition concerning minors or where in the courts below the title used has been such as to conceal the identity of one or more parties to the action, this fact should be clearly drawn to the attention of the Judicial Office at the time the petition is lodged, so that the title adopted in the House of Lords may take due account of the need to protect the identity of the minors or parties in question.

Designation of Prosecutor

4.5   The prosecuting authority should be cited as follows: 'Director of Public Prosecutions [or other prosecuting authority] (on behalf of Her Majesty)'.

Service

4.6   A copy of the petition must be served on the respondents or their agents, either by delivery in person or by first class post, before lodgment in the Judicial Office. A certificate of such service must be endorsed on the back of the original petition and signed. In habeas corpus matters concerned with extradition, the petition must be served on the government seeking extradition or upon the Director of Public Prosecutions if he is acting for that government.

Lodgment

4.7   The original petition must be lodged in the Judicial Office together with a copy of the order appealed from and, if separate, a copy of the order of the court below certifying the point of law and refusing leave to appeal to the House of Lords. If the order is not immediately available, the petition should be lodged in time and the order lodged as soon as possible thereafter.

4.8   An agent who attends the Judicial Office to lodge papers must be familiar with the subject matter of the petition.

4.9   Once lodged, the petition will be presented to the House and recorded in the Minutes of Proceedings.

Appearance for respondents

4.10   Respondents or their agents should enter appearance to a petition for leave as soon as they have received service. They should enter their name and address at the Judicial Office, either in person or by post. Those respondents who intend to take no part in the proceedings before the House should notify the Judicial Office, in writing, of that fact. Communications concerning the petition will be sent only to those who have entered appearance. An order for costs will not be made in favour of a respondent who has not entered appearance.

5.   APPEAL COMMITTEE

5.1   On presentation to the House, a petition for leave to appeal will be referred to an Appeal Committee.

Additional papers
5.2   The following additional papers, for use by the Appeal Committee, must be lodged within one week of lodgment of the petition:
    (a)   four copies of the petition;
    (b)   four copies of the order appealed from;
    (c)   if separate, four copies of the order of the court certifying the point of law and refusing leave to appeal to the House of Lords;
    (d)   five copies of the official transcript of the judgment of the court below;
    (e)   five copies of the order of the court of first instance;
    (f)   five copies of the official transcript of the judgment of the court of first instance or of the case stated;
    (g)   one copy of any other document considered necessary.
The Court of Appeal (Criminal Division) may make arrangements for the copying of certain of the above documents upon application to the Registrar.

Admissibility of petitions
5.3   The Appeal Committee will consider whether the petition is admissible and, if so, whether it should be dismissed, provisionally allowed or referred for an oral hearing.
5.4   If the members of the Appeal Committee are unanimously of the opinion that a petition is not admissible, parties will be notified that the petition is dismissed.

Respondents' objections
5.5   If the Appeal Committee takes the provisional view that leave to appeal should be given or given upon terms, the respondents will be invited to lodge objections to the petition, briefly setting out reasons why the petition should not be allowed or making other relevant submissions as to the terms upon which leave should be granted. If objections are submitted they must be served on the other parties. The petitioner will be notified of any proposed terms and may be invited to submit observations on the respondents' objections. If written observations are submitted they must be served on the respondents.
5.6   Parties invited to submit either objections or observations will be informed of the date by which they may do so. Seven copies should be lodged in the Judicial Office by that date. The Judicial Office should be informed by the same date if no such submissions are to be made.
5.7   If, having considered any objections submitted by the respondents, the Appeal Committee is unanimous that leave to appeal should be given, parties will be notified of that result.
5.8   Where the Appeal Committee is not unanimous, or where further argument is required, the petition will be referred for an oral hearing.

Oral hearing
5.9   If a petition is referred for an oral hearing, the petitioners and all respondents who have entered appearance will be notified of the probable date of meeting of the

Appeal Committee, before whom the parties are directed to attend. However, no guarantee can be given that the date notified will be adhered to. Once referred for an oral hearing, a petition may be listed at any time, possibly at short notice.

5.10   Parties may be heard before the Appeal Committee by counsel, by agent, or in person, but only one may be heard on each side. Only junior counsel's fees are allowed on taxation for this or any other stage of the petition for leave procedure.

5.11   If counsel is briefed, the Judicial Office must be notified of the name.

5.12   Authorities should not normally be cited before the Appeal Committee.

Appeal Committee order

5.13   Copies of the Minutes of Proceedings of the House recording the decision of the Appeal Committee are sent to all parties.

5.14   A formal order of the Appeal Committee is only issued on written request, and on payment of a fee. An Appeal Committee order is not required for taxation of costs in the House of Lords.

6.   COSTS

6.1   Where a petition for leave to appeal is determined without an oral hearing, costs may be awarded as follows:

(a)   to a legally aided petitioner, reasonable costs incurred in preparing papers for the Appeal Committee;

(b)   to a legally aided respondent, only those costs necessarily incurred in attending the client, attending the petitioner's agents, perusing the petition, entering appearance and, where applicable, preparing respondent's objections to the petition;

(c)   to an unassisted respondent where the petitioner is legally aided, payment out of the Legal Aid Fund (subject to section 19 of the Legal Aid Act 1988) of costs as specified at (b) above;

(d)   to a petitioner or respondent, payment out of central funds, pursuant to section 16 or section 17 of the Prosecution of Offences Act 1985, of costs incurred at (a) or (b) above, as the case may be;

(e)   where neither party is legally aided, respondents may apply for their costs at (b) above to be paid by the petitions.

6.2   Where costs are sought under (c), (d) or (e) above, application must be made in writing to the Judicial Office before the bill is lodged.

6.3   Where a petition for leave to appeal is referred for an oral hearing and is dismissed, application for costs must be made by the respondent at the end of the hearing, before the Bar is finally cleared. No order for costs will be made unless requested at that time.

6.4   Where a petition for leave to appeal is allowed, costs of the petition will be costs in the ensuing appeal.

6.5   Bills of costs for taxation must be lodged within three months from the date of the decision of the Appeal Committee or the date on which a petition for leave is withdrawn. If an extension of the three month period is required, application should be made to the Taxing Officer in writing before the original time expires. If no application is made a bill lodged out of time will be accepted only in exceptional circumstances.

6.6   The directions relating to taxation, and the form of bill to be lodged, are available on request from the Judicial Office.

7. FEES

7.1   No fee is payable at any stage of a petition for leave to appeal, except when an Appeal Committee order is requested. Fees are payable on the taxation of a bill of costs.

II. APPEALS

8. TIME LIMITS

8.1   In cases where the court below has granted leave to appeal to the House of Lords, the petition of appeal must be lodged within three months of the date of the order appealed from. This time limit may be extended on reasoned request made within time, at the direction of the Principal Clerk. Appellants are, however, recommended to observe the time limit applicable to civil appeals.

8.2   When leave to appeal is granted by the House, the Appeal Committee may set a time limit within which the petition of appeal must be lodged. If no such limit is set, the recommendation of Direction 8.1 should be observed.

9. USE OF LONDON AGENTS

9.1   Solicitors outside London may appoint London agents. Those who decide not to do so should note that any additional costs incurred as a result of that decision may be disallowed on taxation.

10. LODGMENT OF APPEAL

Form of petition of appeal

10.1   All formal documents should be produced on good quality A4 paper, bound on the left and using both sides of the paper. For form of petition, see Appendix C; for preparation of documents, see Direction 28.

10.2   A petition of appeal must be signed by the appellants or their agents.

Title and designation of prosecutor

10.3   Petitions of Appeal to the House of Lords carry the same title as the cause in the court below. 'Regina' is used in the title and is always given first. The parties are described as appellants and respondents. In the petition the prosecuting authority should be cited as follows: 'Director of Public Prosecutions [or other prosecuting authority] (on behalf of Her Majesty).'

Appeals involving minors

10.4   In any appeal concerning minors or where in the courts below the title used has been such as to conceal the identity of one or more parties to the action, this fact should be clearly drawn to the attention of the Judicial Office at the time the appeal is lodged, so that the title adopted in the House of Lords may take due account of the need to protect the identity of the minors or parties in question.

In any appeal concerning minors, parties should also consider whether it would be appropriate for the House to make an order under section 39 of the Children and Young Persons Act 1933 and should, in any event, inform the Judicial Office if such an order has been made by a court below. A request for such an order should be made in writing, preferably on behalf of all parties to the appeal, as soon as possible after the appeal has been presented and not later than two weeks before the commencement of the hearing.

Service

10.5   A copy of the petition must be served on the respondents or their agents, either by delivery in person or by first class post. A certificate of such service must be endorsed on the back of the original petition and signed. (For form of certificate, see Appendix C.)

Lodgment of Appeal

10.6   The original petition of appeal together with five copies must be lodged in the Judicial Office.

Appearance for Respondents

10.7   Respondents' agents should enter appearance to an appeal as soon as they have received service of the petition of appeal. They should enter their name and address at the Judicial Office, either in person or by post. Those respondents who intend to take no part in the proceedings before the House should notify the Judicial Office, in writing, of that fact. Communications concerning the appeal will be sent only to those who have entered appearance.

11.   SECURITY FOR COSTS AND FEES

11.1   No security for costs is required to be lodged in criminal appeals to the House of Lords, and no fees are payable, except on taxation.

12.   STATEMENT OF FACTS AND ISSUES

12.1   The appellant must prepare a statement of the facts and issues involved in the appeal. The appellants should draw up the statement and submit it to the respondents for discussion. Wherever possible, the statement lodged should be a single document agreed between the parties. It should not contain material more appropriately included in a case.

12.2   Where, after consultation, the parties are unable to adopt an agreed statement, the respondents may prepare their own statement which should be appended to that of the appellant under the title 'Respondents statement of facts and issues'. If the respondents neither agree to a joint statement nor produce a statement of their own for attachment to the appellant's statement, the appellant may lodge his statement with a certificate to the effect that the respondents have been offered an opportunity to join in preparation of the statement.

12.3   The statement need not set out or summarise the judgments of the lower courts, nor set out statutory provisions, nor contain an account of the proceedings below. It may be assumed that the statement will be read in conjunction with the documents in the appendix. Moreover, attention is drawn to the remarks of Lord Diplock in *M V Yorke Motors* v *Edwards* [1982] 1 WLR 444, [1982] 1 All ER 1024.

12.4   In any appeal under the Criminal Appeal Act 1968, the statement must clearly state whether any grounds of appeal have been undetermined by the Court of Appeal. See also Direction 15.5.

12.5   For form of statement, see Direction 28.

13.   APPENDIX

13.1   The appellants must also prepare and lodge an appendix containing documents used in evidence or recording proceedings in the courts below. This should be done in consultation with the respondents, and the contents of the appendix must be agreed between the parties.

13.2   The cost of preparing the appendix is borne in the first instance by the appellant, though it will ultimately be subject to the decision of the House as to the costs of the appeal.

Contents of Appendix

13.3   The appendix should contain only such documents, or such extracts from documents, as are clearly necessary for the support and understanding of the argument of the appeal. No document which was not used in evidence or does not record proceedings relevant to the action in the courts below may be included. Authorities must not be included except after consultation with the Judicial Office.

13.4   The appendix may consist of one or more parts. Part I should contain:

    (a)   formal originating documents, summonses, indictments etc;

    (b)   case stated (if any);

    (c)   judgments of the courts at first instance and on appeal together with copies of the orders of all courts (in magistrates' courts, a memorandum of conviction; in the Crown Court, a certificate of conviction);

    (d)   the relevant statutory provisions including Statutory Instruments.

For judgments published in the Law Reports or the Weekly Law Reports, the relevant unbound parts should be included, if available; otherwise the All England Reports may be used. Where at the time of preparation of the appendix a judgment of a court below is not published in one of the reports listed above, a transcript must be

included. If it then becomes available by the time the bound case is lodged, the published version should be substituted for the transcript. Where a judgment is published after the lodging of the bound case but before the hearing of the appeal, six copies should be submitted to the Judicial Office as soon as possible. Judgments in draft are not accepted. For statutes, the printed Act or set of Regulations should be used if it is conveniently small; if not, the relevant provisions only should be copied.
13.5   Other documents should be included in Part II of the appendix (and subsequent parts if, owing to bulk, the material is more conveniently made up into more than one volume).
13.6   For form of appendix, see Direction 28.

Documents in readiness at hearing
13.7   Any documents disputed between the parties, and any documents which are not included in the appendix but which may be required at the hearing, should be held in readiness and, subject to leave being given, may be introduced at an appropriate moment. Six copies are required. The other parties must be given notice of any documents which will be held in readiness at the hearing.

Respondents' additional documents
13.8   Where the appellants decline to include in the appendix any documents which the respondents consider necessary for their argument of the appeal, the respondents must prepare and reproduce them at their own cost. The respondents' additional documents must be produced in the same form as, and paginated consecutively with, the appendix. The costs of such preparation will ultimately be subject to the decision of the House as to the costs of the appeal.

Examination of Appendix
13.9   The appendix (and, where applicable, respondents' additional documents) is for the use of all parties. As soon as a proof is available it should be examined against the originals by all parties, if possible at one joint examination.
13.10   As soon as practicable after the examination a final proof of the appendix and any additional documents should be provided to each party.

14.   LODGMENT OF STATEMENT AND APPENDIX

14.1   Unless otherwise ordered, the statement must be lodged within six weeks of the presentation of the petition of appeal. This time limit may be extended on reasoned request made within time, at the direction of the Principal Clerk. The appendix (and, where applicable, respondents' additional documents) should be lodged at the same time. The appellants should deposit in the Judicial Office six copies of the statement, six copies of Part 1 of the appendix (including any additional documents), and 15 copies of each subsequent part of the appendix (including any additional documents).

15.   APPELLANTS' AND RESPONDENTS' CASES

15.1   No later than two weeks before the proposed date of hearing, the appellants and respondents should lodge their own cases. In certain circumstances, the Principal Clerk may direct that cases need not be lodged.

15.2   A case should be a succinct statement of a party's argument in the appeal. It should omit the material contained in the statement of facts and issues and should be confined to the heads of argument which counsel propose to submit at the hearing.

15.3   If either party is abandoning any point taken below, this should be made plain in the case. Equally if they intend to apply in the course of the hearing for leave to introduce a new point not taken below, this should be indicated in their case and the Judicial Office should be informed. If such a point involves the introduction of fresh evidence, application for leave must be made either in the case or by lodging a petition for leave to adduce the fresh evidence.

15.4   If the parties intend to invite the House to depart from one of its own decisions, this intention must be clearly stated in a separate paragraph of the case, to which special attention must be drawn. The intention must also be restated as one of the reasons. A respondent who wishes to contend that a decision of the court below should be affirmed on grounds other than those relied on by that Court, must set out the grounds for that contention in the case.

15.5   In any appeal under the Criminal Appeal Act 1968 in which grounds of appeal have been undetermined by the Court of Appeal (see Direction 12.4 above), each party should include in their case submissions on the merits of those grounds and on how they would seek to have them disposed of by the House.

15.6   All cases must conclude with a numbered summary of the reasons upon which the argument is founded, and must bear the signature of at least one counsel who has appeared in the court below or who will be briefed for the hearing before the House.

15.7   Counsel should take note of the speech of Lord Diplock in *Roberts Petroleum Limited* v *Bernard Kenny* [1983] 2 AC 192 as to the citing of unreported cases. Leave to cite unreported cases should be sought at the hearing and will 'only be granted upon counsel giving an assurance that the transcript contains a statement of some principle of law, relevant to an issue in the appeal to [the] House, that is binding upon the Court of Appeal and of which the substance, as distinct from the mere choice of phraseology, is not to be found in any judgment of that court that has appeared in one of the generalised or specialised series of reports' (*ibid*, p. 202). Unreported cases should not be included in documents lodged.

15.8   The lodgment of a case carries the right to be heard by two counsel, one of whom may be leading counsel. Unless otherwise ordered upon application at the hearing, only two counsel's fees are allowed on taxation.

Separate cases

15.9   All the appellants must join in one case, and all the respondents must similarly join unless it can be shown that the interests of one or more of the respondents are distinct from those of the remainder. In the latter event, the respondents' agents first lodging their case must give a certificate by letter in one of the following forms:

(a) 'We, as agents for the respondent(s) [name particular parties], certify that opportunity has been offered by us for joining in one case to the respondent(s) [name particular parties] whose interests are, in our opinion, similar to those set out in the case lodged by us.'

(b) 'We, as agents for the respondent(s) [name particular parties], certify that the interests represented in the case lodged by us are, in our opinion, distinct from those of the remaining respondent(s).'

15.10 When one of the foregoing certificates has been given, all remaining respondents wishing to lodge a case must respectively petition to do so in respect of each of their separate cases. Such petitions must be consented to by the appellants, and must set out the reasons for separate lodgment.

Joint cases

15.11 The lodgment of a joint case on behalf of both appellants and respondents may be permitted in certain circumstances.

Lodgment of cases

15.12 Each party must lodge in the Judicial Office six copies of their case.

Exchange of cases

15.13 As soon as the cases have been prepared, all parties must exchange cases. The number of cases should be sufficient to meet the requirements of counsel and agents but should not usually exceed eight.

16.   BOUND VOLUMES

16.1 As soon as cases have been exchanged, and in any event no later than one week before the proposed date of hearing, the appellants must lodge (in addition to the documents earlier lodged) 15 bound volumes. Each should contain:

(a)   the petition(s) of appeal;

(b)   the statement of facts and issues;

(c)   the appellants' and respondents' cases;

(d)   Part I of the appendix;

(e)   respondents' additional documents (if any and if supplementary to Part I of the appendix).

16.2 For form of bound volumes, see Direction 28.

16.3 To enable the appellants to lodge the bound volumes, the respondents must provide them with 15 further copies of their case and, where applicable, with 15 further copies of the additional documents.

16.4 Respondents should arrange with the appellants for the binding of such volumes as the respondents' counsel and agents may require.

17.   SETTING DOWN FOR HEARING

17.1   As soon as the statement and appendix have been lodged, the appellants must apply to set the appeal down for hearing.

Time Estimates
17.2   Within seven days of the setting down of the appeal, each party should notify the Judicial Office of the time, in hours, which counsel consider necessary for each address which it is proposed should be made on behalf of that party.
17.3   Subject to any directions which may be given at or prior to the hearing counsel will be expected to confine the length of their submissions to the time indicated in the estimates. Arrangements for hearings will be made on that basis.

18.   NOTICE OF HEARING

18.1   In arranging the dates for the hearing of an appeal the Judicial Office will endeavour to suit the convenience of all parties, and to that end provisional dates are arranged some time in advance. However, no guarantee can be given that these dates will be adhered to and once an appeal has been set down it may be called in at any time, possibly at short notice. Counsel, agents and parties should, in any event, hold themselves in readiness during the week prior to, and the week following, the provisional date arranged.
18.2   Agents receive formal notification shortly before the hearing.
18.3   The Judicial Office must be informed as early as possible of the names of counsel briefed.

19.   AUTHORITIES

19.1   At least a week before the hearing of the appeal, agents for all parties should forward to the Judicial Office a list, drawn up by junior counsel, of the law reports, text books and other authorities on which they rely.
19.2   The list should be in two parts. Part I should contain only those authorities which counsel definitely intend to cite before the House. Copies of these authorities will be made available to each member of the Appellate Committee at the hearing. Part II should contain any authorities which in the opinion of counsel might be called for in the course of the appeal but which counsel themselves do not intend to cite. Copies of these will be available only to the chairman of the committee.
19.3   Lists should indicate by reference those particular passages of the authorities on which counsel rely.
19.4   Where a case is not reported in the Law Reports, references to other recognised reports should be given.
19.5   The House of Lords Library can arrange for copies of certain authorities to be made available at the hearing. Parties must themselves provide six copies of any

other authority or of unreported cases. They must similarly provide copies of any authority of which adequate notice has not been given.

19.6   In certain circumstances parties may prefer to provide photocopies of all their authorities. In that event, the particular passages relied on should be indicated by highlighting. Parties are requested to use small, flexible covers in preference to heavy binders.

19.7   It is the responsibility of each party to ensure that all other parties to the appeal are provided with copies of any authority, bundle of authorities or other document to which reference may be made at the hearing.

20.   COSTS

Submissions at the hearing
20.1   If counsel wish to seek an order other than that costs be awarded to the successful party or, where the successful party is statute barred from an award of costs, no order for costs, submissions to that effect should be made at the hearing immediately after the conclusion of the argument.

Submissions at judgment
20.2   Leave may be given to a party to make such submissions at the judgment in the House. Prior notice of intention to make submissions on costs must be given in writing to the Judicial Office, at least two clear days before the judgment, stating the nature of the order sought. A copy of the submissions must be sent to the agents for the other party or parties to the appeal.

21.   JUDGMENT

21.1   Agents will be notified of the date of judgment, which is delivered in the Chamber of the House. Only one junior counsel for each party or group of parties who have lodged a case is required to attend when judgment is delivered, and only a junior's fee will be allowed on taxation. If leading counsel wish to attend judgment, it is the convention that Queen's Counsel wear full-bottomed wigs when appearing at the Bar of the House.

21.2   The opinions of the Lords of Appeal may be made available to each party a short while before judgment is given, usually at 10.30 am when judgment is to be given at 2.00 pm. In that event, a strict embargo applies until after judgment has been delivered.

22.   ORDER OF THE HOUSE

Draft order
22.1   After the House has given judgment, drafts of the order of the House are sent to all parties who lodged a case. The drafts must be returned to the Judicial Office within one week of the date of receipt (unless otherwise directed) either approved or

with suggested amendments. If substantial amendments are proposed, they must be submitted to the agents for the other parties, who should indicate their approval or disagreement, both to the agents submitting the proposals and to the Judicial Office. Where the amendments proposed are contrary to the questions put to the House, a petition should be lodged.

Final order
22.2   One final order, certified by the Clerk of the Parliaments, is sent to the agent for the successful party.
22.3   Prints of the final order are sent free of charge to the agents for all parties who have entered appearance.

23.   BILLS OF COSTS

23.1   Bills of costs for taxation must be lodged within three months from the date of the final judgment or the decision of the Appeal Committee. If an extension of the three-month period is required, application should be made to the Taxing Officer in writing before the original time expires. If no application is made a bill lodged out of time will be accepted only in exceptional circumstances.
23.2   The directions relating to taxation, and the form of bill to be lodged, are available on request from the Judicial Office.

III.   MISCELLANEOUS

24.   LEGAL AID

24.1   The House of Lords does not grant legal aid. Except in respect of appeals from a Divisional Court of the Queen's Bench Division, application must be made to the Court from whose decision the appeal is made.
24.2   In the case of appeals from a Divisional Court of the Queen's Bench Division, application for legal aid should be made to the appropriate Area Office of the Legal Aid Board or, in Northern Ireland, to the Legal Aid Committee. Where such an application has not been determined within the statutory fourteen days (see Direction 3.2), the petition must incorporate an application for an extension of time (see Direction 3.3). The fact that legal aid was applied for should be given as a reason for the petition being outside the statutory fourteen-day period. Such a petition should, if at all possible, be lodged within fourteen days of the final determination of the legal aid application.
24.3   A copy of any legal aid certificate must be lodged in the Judicial Office.

25.   CONSOLIDATION AND CONJOINDER

25.1   Where the issues in two or more appeals are similar, it may be appropriate for them to be consolidated or conjoined. Consolidation of two or more appeals results in them being carried on as a single cause with one set of counsel and one case on each side and a single appendix. Conjoinder is a looser linking of two or more appeals, and a number of variations are possible. The Judicial Office should be consulted on the question of whether consolidation or some form of conjoinder is most likely to be appropriate. A principal consideration should be to avoid, wherever possible, separate representation by counsel or any duplication in the submissions made.

25.2   Applications to consolidate or to conjoin appeals and other incidental applications must be made by petition. All parties should ensure that their requirements are covered by the petition.

25.3   The petition should be signed by the agents for all petitioners and must be submitted to the agents for all the other parties who have entered appearance for the endorsement of their consent. If consent is refused, the petition must be endorsed with a certificate that it has been served on the agents in question.

25.4   If all parties consent to or join in the petition, one copy only of the petition should be lodged. If any party refuses their consent, six copies of the petition should be lodged. In that event the petition will be referred to an Appeal Committee.

26.   OPPOSED INCIDENTAL PETITIONS

26.1   Unless the Principal Clerk directs otherwise, opposed incidental petitions (including any interlocutory petition which relates to any petition of appeal) will be referred to an Appeal Committee.

26.2   Six copies of the petition must be lodged. The original petition should bear a certificate of service on the other parties.

26.3   If an oral hearing is ordered, the parties may apply at that time to hand in affidavits and such other documents as they may wish. Six copies will be required. Copies of such documents must be served on the other parties before the oral hearing.

27.   BAIL

27.1   The House of Lords does not grant bail. Applications should be made to the court below. Where bail is granted to a party to an appeal to the House, the Judicial Office should be notified.

27.2   The attendance of a party to an appeal who is in custody, unless required for the purposes of the hearing, will not be permitted. Where the attendance of a party in custody is required, his agents will be informed of that fact in writing.

27.3   It should be noted that where a party was on bail pending the hearing of the appeal, surrender is usually required on the first day of the hearing.

28.   PREPARATION OF DOCUMENTS

General

28.1   Documents which are not clearly legible or which are not produced in the form specified will not be accepted.

28.2   The Judicial Office can give advice as to the form and content of documents for lodging. Parties are advised to consult the Office at all stages of preparation and should submit proofs for approval where appropriate.

28.3   Appendix E shows the numbers of documents usually required for the hearing of an appeal.

28.4   All formal documents should be produced on good quality A4 paper, bound on the left and using both sides of the paper. Original petitions should be sewn.

Form of statement and case

28.5   The statement and case should be produced with letters down the inside margin. The outside margin should carry references to the relevant pages of the appendix.

28.6   The front page of the statement should carry the references of every law report of the cause in the courts below. A head-note summary should be given, whether or not the cause has been reported.

28.7   The front page of the statement should carry an indication of the time occupied by the cause in each court below.

28.8   The statement should be signed by counsel on both sides, and their names clearly indicated. Where the statement is not agreed to by all parties it should be signed by counsel for the appellants and should indicate that the respondents have been given due facilities for joining in the statement.

28.9   Each party's case should be signed by their counsel.

Form of Appendix

28.10   The appendix should be bound with plastic comb binding and in red covers of Fibrex board.

28.11   All documents must be numbered and each part of the appendix must contain a list of its contents.

28.12   Documents should be reproduced economically and in the minimum numbers necessary for the purposes of the appeal.

28.13   Documents of an unsuitable size or form for binding with the other documents (such as maps or booklets) should be inserted in pockets at the back of the appropriate volume.

Form of bound volumes

28.14   The bound volumes should be bound in the same manner as the appendix. They should contain cut-out indices for each of the items listed in Direction 16.1, tabbed with the name of the document on the front sheet of each. The front cover should carry a list of the contents and the names of the agents for all parties. The short title of the cause should be given on a strip affixed to the plastic spine. Each volume should include a few blank pages at either end.

29. DISPOSAL OF DOCUMENTS

29.1   All petitions and supporting documents lodged become the property of the House. However, if application is made in writing within fourteen days of the determination of an appeal, or a petition for leave to appeal, documents other than the original petition may, at the direction of the Principal Clerk, be returned to the parties.

30. LODGMENT

30.1   'Lodgment' and 'lodging' mean delivery to a member of the Judicial Office staff, either in person during opening hours or by post. Where the time for lodging a document expires on a Saturday, Sunday, Bank Holiday or any other day on which the Judicial Office is closed, it will be received if it is lodged on the first day on which the Office is next open.

30.2   Communications may be transmitted by facsimile, and the cost of such transmission will be allowed on taxation, only where urgent circumstances make this appropriate. No document which is to be presented to the House may be so transmitted.

30.3   Any agent who attends the Judicial Office to lodge papers must be familiar with the matter to be dealt with.

APPENDIX A

FORM OF PETITION FOR LEAVE TO APPEAL

(SEE DIRECTION 4)

IN THE HOUSE OF LORDS

ON APPEAL FROM HER MAJESTY'S COURT OF APPEAL (CRIMINAL DIVISION)/A DIVISIONAL COURT OF THE QUEEN'S BENCH DIVISION **[or the relevant court]**

BETWEEN:
                    [Set out title of cause.]

TO THE RIGHT HONOURABLE THE HOUSE OF LORDS

THE HUMBLE PETITION OF **[set out full name(s) and address(es) of petitioner(s)]** PRAYING FOR LEAVE TO APPEAL IN ACCORDANCE WITH THE CRIMINAL APPEAL ACT 1968/ADMINISTRATION OF JUSTICE ACT 1960 **[or the relevant statute]** SHEWETH—

   1. That **[set out briefly in numbered paragraphs such facts and arguments as may be necessary to enable the Appeal Committee to report to the House whether leave to appeal should be granted].**

YOUR PETITIONER(S) HUMBLY SUBMIT(S) that leave to appeal to your Lordships' House should be granted for the following among other

REASONS

[Here give numbered reasons, generally summarising the foregoing argu-ments.]

And your petitioner(s) will ever pray.

                              [Signature of petitioner(s) or agents.]

FORM OF BACK OF PETITION FOR LEAVE TO APPEAL, SHOWING CERTIFICATE OF SERVICE TO BE ENDORSED ON ORIGINAL PETITION

I/We, (Messrs.) **[name]**, of **[address]**, (agents for) the petitioner(s) within-named, hereby certify that on the ... day of .... 19... we served (Messrs. **[name]** of **[address]**, agents for) **[name(s) of respondent(s)]**, the within-named respondent(s), with a correct copy of the aforegoing petition and with notice that the petition for leave to appeal would be presented to the House of Lords on behalf of the petitioner(s) as soon as conveniently may be.

IN THE HOUSE OF LORDS

ON APPEAL FROM **[name court]**

BETWEEN:

[Set out title of cause.]

PETITION FOR LEAVE TO APPEAL

[Signature of petitioner(s) or agents.]

[Set out full name, address, telephone number, and reference (if any) of petitioner(s) or agents]

APPENDIX B

FORM OF PETITION FOR LEAVE TO APPEAL OUT OF TIME

(SEE DIRECTION 3.3)

IN THE HOUSE OF LORDS

ON APPEAL FROM HER MAJESTY'S COURT OF APPEAL (CRIMINAL DIVISION)/A DIVISIONAL COURT OF THE QUEEN'S BENCH DIVISION **[or the relevant court]**

BETWEEN:
                                [Set out title of cause.]

TO THE RIGHT HONOURABLE THE HOUSE OF LORDS

THE HUMBLE PETITION OF **[set out full name(s) and address(es) of petitioner(s)]** PRAYING FOR AN EXTENSION OF TIME WITHIN WHICH THE PETITION MAY BE LODGED AND FOR LEAVE TO APPEAL IN ACCORDANCE WITH THE CRIMINAL APPEAL ACT 1968/ADMINIS-TRATION OF JUSTICE ACT 1960 **[or the relevant statute]**.

Your Petitioner(s) humbly pray(s) that, in accordance with Section 34(2)/Section 2(3) **[or relevant provision]** of that Act, your Lordships will be pleased to grant him/her/them an extension of time to enable this Petition to be considered. The Petition is out of time for the following reasons:

That **[set out briefly the reasons why the petition was not lodged in time]**.

THE HUMBLE PETITION SHEWETH—

1. That **[continue as indicated in Appendix A]**.

APPENDIX C
FORM OF PETITION OF APPEAL

(SEE DIRECTION 10)

IN THE HOUSE OF LORDS

ON APPEAL FROM HER MAJESTY'S COURT OF APPEAL (CRIMINAL DIVISION)/A DIVISIONAL COURT OF THE QUEEN'S BENCH DIVISION **[or the relevant court]**

BETWEEN:
[Set out title of cause.]

TO THE RIGHT HONOURABLE THE HOUSE OF LORDS

THE HUMBLE PETITION AND APPEAL OF **[set out the full name(s) and address(es) of the appellant(s)]**

YOUR PETITIONER(S) has/have, in pursuance of section 1 of the Administration of Justice Act 1960/section 33 of the Criminal Appeal Act 1968 **[or the relevant statutory provision]** obtained the Certificate of **[name court below]** set out in the Schedule hereto that the decision of that Court involves a point of law of general public importance.

[EITHER:]

By an Order of the ... day of .... 19..., the **[name court below]** gave Your Petitioner(s) leave to appeal from the said decision.

[OR:]

Your Lordships gave Your Petitioner(s) leave to appeal from the said decision on the ... day of .... 19....

YOUR PETITIONER(S) humbly pray(s) that the matter of the Order set forth in the Schedule hereto may be revised before Her Majesty the Queen, in Her Court of Parliament, and that the said Order may be reversed, varied or altered or that your Petitioner(s) may have such other relief in the premises as to Her Majesty the Queen, in Her Court of Parliament, may seem meet.

[Signature(s) of appellant(s) or agents]

THE SCHEDULE ABOVE REFERRED TO

from HER MAJESTY'S COURT OF APPEAL (CRIMINAL DIVISION)/A DIVISIONAL COURT OF THE QUEEN'S BENCH DIVISION **[or other court].**

[Add here, if appropriate (see below), the words: FIRST SCHEDULE.]

In the matter of certain criminal proceedings wherein .... was the Prosecutor and .... was the Defendant.

The order of **[state court]** of **[date of order]** appealed from is/are in the words following, the portions complained of being underlined:

[Set out here the whole of the order, with all and only those parts complained of underlined. The recital, the certified point of law and any decision on an application for leave to appeal to the House of Lords should be included but should not be underlined.]

[Where a certificate has been granted and a decision on an application for leave to appeal made by a subsequent order of the court, the words 'FIRST SCHEDULE' should appear where indicated above and the following should be added:]

SECOND SCHEDULE

The order of **[state court]** of **[date of order]**, by which that court granted/refused leave to appeal and certified that a point of law of general public importance was involved in the aforesaid decision, is in the words following:

[Set out here the whole of the order, including the recital.]

FORM OF BACK OF PETITION OF APPEAL, SHOWING CERTIFICATE OF SERVICE TO BE ENDORSED ON ORIGINAL PETITION

I/We, (Messrs.) **[name]**, of **[address]**, (agents for) the appellant(s) within-named, hereby certify that on the ... day of .... 19... I/we served (Messrs. **[name]**, of **[address]**, agents for) **[name(s) of respondent(s)]**, the within-named respondent(s), with a correct copy of the aforegoing appeal and with notice that the petition of appeal would be presented to the House of Lords on behalf of the appellant(s) as soon as conveniently may be.

[Signature of appellant(s) or agents.]

IN THE HOUSE OF LORDS

ON APPEAL FROM **[name court]**

BETWEEN:

[Set out title of cause.]

_____

PETITION OF APPEAL

_____

[Set out full name, address, telephone number and reference (if any) of appellant(s) or agents]

APPENDIX D

FORM OF PETITION FOR CONSOLIDATION/CONJOINDER

(SEE DIRECTION 25)

IN THE HOUSE OF LORDS

ON APPEAL FROM HER MAJESTY'S COURT OF APPEAL (CRIMINAL DIVISION)/A DIVISIONAL COURT OF THE QUEEN'S BENCH DIVISION **[or the relevant court]**

BETWEEN: ....

                               and

                               ....

AND BETWEEN:

                               ....

                               and

                               ....

TO THE RIGHT HONOURABLE THE HOUSE OF LORDS

THE HUMBLE PETITION OF **[set out full name(s) of appellant(s)]** SHEWETH—

That your petitioner(s) presented (a) petition(s) of appeal on the ... day of .... 19.... complaining of (an) order(s) of the **[name relevant court below]** dated the ... day of .... 19....

That your petitioner(s) **[name appellant(s) in other appeal(s), if different]** presented (a) petition(s) of appeal on the ... day of .... 19.... complaining of (an) order(s) of the **[name relevant court below]** dated the ... day .... of 19....

That the same matters of law are raised in each of the appeals (and that the appeals of **[name relevant parties]** to **[name relevant court below]** were heard and argued together and one judgment was delivered in respect of the (two) appeals).

That it is expedient that your petitioners' said appeals be consolidated/ conjoined.

YOUR PETITIONER(S) THEREFORE HUMBLY PRAY(S)

[Consolidation:]

That the said appeals may be consolidated and that he/she/they be allowed to lodge (one) separate statement(s), one case and one appendix in respect of the **[insert relevant number]** appeals and that the respondent(s) have leave to lodge one case in respect of the appeals.

[Conjoinder:]

That the said appeals may be conjoined and that they be allowed to lodge separate statements and cases and one appendix in respect of the **[insert relevant number]** appeals and that the respondents have leave to lodge separate cases in respect of the appeals or that such other order may be made with a view to the convenient conduct of the said appeals as to your Lordships may seem meet.

And your petitioner(s) will ever pray.

[Signature of petitioner(s) or their agents]

(Agents for the) Petitioner(s)

[Signature of other appellant(s) or their agents]

(Agents for the) Co-Petitioner(s)

[etc]

[Where one or more respondent(s) consent(s) to consolidation/conjoinder, the following should be added:]

We consent to the prayer of the above petition.

[Signature of respondent(s) to first appeal or their agents]

(Agents for the) Respondents **[name relevant respondent(s)]**

[Signature of respondent(s) to second appeal or their agents]

(Agents for the) Respondents **[name relevant respondent(s)]**

[etc]

[Where one or more respondent(s) do not consent, the following should be added:]

I/We, (Messrs.) **[name]**, of **[address]**, (agents for) the above-named petitioner(s), hereby certify that the above-named respondent(s) **[or name relevant respondent(s)]**, has/have been offered the opportunity to join in or consent to the prayer of the above petition.

[Signature of petitioner(s) or their agents]

(Agents for the) Petitioner(s)

APPENDIX E

NUMBER OF DOCUMENTS NORMALLY REQUIRED FOR THE HEARING OF AN APPEAL

The numbers shown below are the minimum specifically laid down in the Directions. Actual requirements must be subject to agreement and will depend on the number of parties, counsel and agents concerned, and on the special circumstances of each appeal. Copies for the use of the party originating the documents are in addition to the numbers indicated.

APPELLANTS MUST PROVIDE:

		Judicial Office	*Respondent*
(1)	Petition of Appeal	Original and 5 on lodgment; 15 in bound volumes	2 on service
(2)	Statement	6 on setting down; 15 in bound volumes	As arranged
(3)	Case	6 on lodgment; 15 in bound volumes	As arranged on exchange
(4)	Appendix Part I	6 on setting down; 15 in bound volumes	1 in advance; otherwise as arranged
(5)	Appendix Part II and subsequent Parts	15 on setting down	1 in advance; otherwise as arranged
(6)	Bound Volumes	15 after exchange of cases	As arranged

RESPONDENTS MUST PROVIDE:

		Judicial Office	*Appellant*
(1)	Case	6 on lodgment	As arranged on exchange; 15 for bound volumes
(2)	Respondents' additional documents (if any)	6 (if supplementary to Part I of the Appendix); 15 on lodgment (if supplementary to Part II or any other Part of the Appendix)	15 for bound volumes (if supplementary to Part I of Appendix)

APPENDIX F

AUTHORITIES

(SEE DIRECTION 19)

The House of Lords Library has five sets of each of the following authorities:

Law Reports (1866–)
English Reports
Weekly Law Reports
All England Reports
Criminal Appeal Reports
Reports of Patent Cases
Session Cases
Tax Cases
Statutes
European Court Reports
Lloyds Law Reports

The Library has one set of each of the following:

Anglo American Law Review
British Yearbook of International Law
Cambridge Law Journal
Canadian Rights Reporter
Common Market Law Reports
Common Market Law Review
Cox's Criminal Law Cases (1843–1940)
Criminal Appeal Reports (Sentencing)
Criminal Law Review
Crown Office Digest
Estates Gazette Law Reports (1985–)
European Human Rights Law Journal
European Human Rights Law Reports
European Law Digest
European Law Review
Family Law Reports
Financial Law Reports
Fleet Street Reports
Halsburys Laws and Statutes
Housing Law Reports
Human Rights Law Journal
Immigration Appeal Reports

Industrial Cases Reports
Industrial Relations Law Reports
Industrial Tribunal Reports (1966–1978)
International and Comparative Law Quarterly
International Litigation Procedure
Irish Jurist (1848–1866, 1935–1965)
Irish Jurist Reports
Irish Law Reports
Journal of Legal History
Journal of Social Welfare Law
Jurist — Reports of Cases in Law and Equity (1838–1866)
Justice of the Peace Reports
Law Quarterly Review
Law Times Reports
Legislative Studies Quarterly
Local Government Review Reports
Modern Law Review
Northern Ireland Law Reports
Northern Ireland Legal Quarterly (Vol. 34 (1983–)
Northern Ireland Statutes
Oxford Journal of Legal Studies
Planning and Compensation Reports (1963–1967)
Property and Compensation Reports (1968–)
Public Law (British Journal of Administrative Law)
Road Traffic Reports
Rydes Rating Cases (1956–1979)
Scottish Criminal Case Reports (1983–)
Scottish Jurist (1829–1873)
Scottish Law Reporter (1865–1924)
Scottish Law Times
Scottish Planning Law and Practice
Simons Tax Cases (1981–)
Solicitors Journal
Times Law Reports
Weekly Notes (1866–1952)
Weekly Reporter (1852–1906)

13   Criminal Cases Review Commission

INTRODUCTION

The Criminal Cases Review Commission (CCRC) came into being on 31 March 1997. Set up as a result of far-reaching misgivings, following a number of high profile miscarriages of justice, the Commission has power to refer cases to the Crown Court, in the case of magistrates' court convictions and sentences, and the Court of Appeal, in the case of Crown Court matters. The following concentrates solely on the CCRC's powers in respect of magistrates' court convictions.

The CCRC has wider powers than those previously vested in the Home Secretary, and the power to investigate and refer summary convictions and sentences is a new one, presenting a powerful weapon in the defence armoury.

COMMISSION'S CONSTITUTION

The CCRC derives its authority from statute (Criminal Appeal Act 1995), and practitioners are reminded that this part of the appeal process may in itself give rise to a further avenue of challenge, by way of judicial review. The Commission comprises 14 members (its full complement), headed by the chairman, Sir Frederick Crawford, an appointment much criticised due to Sir Frederick's involvement in the higher echelons of Freemasonry. It is regrettably notable that there is an absence of commissioners who can lay claim to having had extensive defence experience, save perhaps Jill Gort who has a record of human rights work. The commissioners are assisted by a team of caseworkers who handle the day-to-day running of the caseload.

JURISDICTION

The CCRC has four distinct functions:

● To refer convictions or sentences of the court to the Crown Court, where it believes that there is a real possibility that the conviction or sentence will not be upheld.

● To assist the Court of Appeal if requested to do so (not applicable to magistrates' court referrals).
● To advise the Home Secretary if requested to do so, in respect of matters in which he is thinking of advising Her Majesty to grant a Royal Pardon.
● The referral of cases to the Home Secretary, where it is felt that a Royal Pardon should be considered.

The question of Royal Pardons is dealt with in a later chapter, although it would appear that the Home Secretary will in future refer all appropriate cases to the Commission.

REFERRALS

The Criminal Appeal Act 1995, s. 11 states:

(1)   Where a person has been convicted of an offence by a magistrates' court in England and Wales, the Commission—
    (a)   may at any time refer the conviction to the Crown Court, and
    (b)   (whether or not they refer the conviction) may at any time refer to the Crown Court any sentence imposed on, or in subsequent proceedings relating to, the conviction.
(2)   A reference under subsection (1) of a person's conviction shall be treated for all purposes as an appeal by the person under section 108(1) of the Magistrates' Courts Act 1980 against the conviction (whether or not he pleaded guilty).
(3)   A reference under subsection (1) of a sentence imposed on, or in subsequent proceedings relating to, a person's conviction shall be treated for all purposes as an appeal by the person under section 108(1) of the Magistrates' Courts Act 1980 against—
    (a)   the sentence, and
    (b)   any other sentence imposed on, or in subsequent proceedings relating to, the conviction or any related conviction.
(4)   On a reference under subsection (1) of a person's conviction the Commission may give notice to the Crown Court that any related conviction which is specified in the notice is to be treated as referred to the Crown Court under subsection (1).
(5)   For the purposes of this section convictions are related if they are convictions of the same person by the same court on the same day.
(6)   On a reference under this section the Crown Court may not award any punishment more severe than that awarded by the court whose decision is referred.
(7)   The Crown Court may grant bail to a person whose conviction or sentence has been referred under this section; and any time during which he is released on bail shall not count as part of any term of imprisonment or detention under his sentence.

Section 11 of the 1995 Act must be read in conjunction with section 13, which lays down restrictions on appealing, namely that in all but exceptional cases, a previous unsuccessful application to the Crown Court must have been made first. It is notable that section 8 allows appeals against conviction irrespective of whether a plea of guilty or not guilty was entered. This modifies the effect of section 108, Magistrates' Courts Act 1980, which only allows such referrals in cases of equivocality. How, then, is one supposed to have had an appeal to the Crown Court refused in such circumstances, in order to invoke the assistance of the CCRC?

As the law stands, new evidence, found after a guilty plea had been tendered, would not allow an appeal to the Crown Court against conviction, but would allow the CCRC to become involved, but for the failure to have an appeal refused in the first place. It must be assumed therefore that the CCRC would regard this as an exceptional reason as to why it should deal with the matter.

MAKING THE APPLICATION

The application is made to the Commission, which is based in Birmingham. The Commission produces and distributes freely an application pack, which includes a standard form of application (reproduced at the end of this chapter). It is imperative that applicants furnish the Commission with the maximum amount of relevant information that is available at the time, and keep the Commission updated on any new developments.

Legal Aid

Legal aid is not available to assist with the making of an application to the Commission. However, legal advice and assistance (the Green Form scheme) is available, provided eligibility limits are met. The Green Form scheme only covers the first two hours of advice, unless an extension is sought from the Legal Aid Board Area Office, or franchisees' devolved powers are used. The Commission's guidance on legal aid, and the Legal Aid Board's latest guidance on the use of devolved powers can be found at the end of the chapter.

Who May Apply?

Any person may invite the Commission to investigate a case, and the Commission can investigate matters of its own motion. This allows for relatives of deceased persons to approach the Commission, and paves the way for a wide variety of miscarriages of justice to be investigated. Recently, for example, the Commission referred the conviction of Derek Bentley to the Court of Appeal. Whilst section 44A(3) of the 1995 Act limits (in applications to the Court of Appeal) the categories of persons approved for appeal purposes, this has no relevance to Crown Court appeals, and there is no corresponding provision. There is no time limit for the making of an appeal by the Commission in these (or indeed any other) circumstances.

Assisting the Commission

The standard application form makes reference to a large number of documents which will generally assist the Commission in reaching a decision. Practitioners can further assist by producing summaries and skeleton arguments for the Commission.

Upon receipt of an application, all the information is scanned onto computer, and the case allocated to a caseworker. Caseworkers work closely with the commissioners throughout the investigations. Powerful software allows for cross-referencing and analysis of large volumes of material.

The quality of the original application can have a very important effect on the quality of the subsequent review of the case.

CRITERIA FOR REVIEW

The Commission can only refer to the Crown Court cases which meet the statutory criteria for referral. A reference of a conviction, verdict, finding or sentence must not be made unless:

● the Commission considers that there is a real possibility that the conviction, verdict, finding or sentence would not be upheld were the reference to be made; and
● the Commission so considers:
(i) in the case of a conviction, verdict or finding, because of an argument, or evidence, not raised in the proceedings which led to it or on any appeal or application for leave to appeal against it, or
(ii) in the case of sentence, because of an argument on a point of law, or information not so raised; *and*
● an appeal against the conviction, verdict, finding or sentence has been determined or leave to appeal against it has been refused; *save that*
● nothing (above) is to prevent the making of a reference if it appears to the Commission that there are exceptional circumstances which justify making it.

The above reflect the criteria in s. 13, Criminal Appeal Act 1995. The Act uses peculiar terminology, and suggests for example that a new argument on a point of law would not be sufficient in the case of an appeal against conviction, but clearly would be in respect of sentence. An appellant's only hope in these circumstances must be that exceptional circumstances could be found. It is accepted that poor legal representation may well amount to an exceptional circumstance. It is clear that the test for the referral of sentences is much more narrowly expressed.

The Test of 'Real Possibility'

There is no statutory definition of the term. During Parliamentary debate the Under-Secretary of State for the Home Department commented:

[that the definition] ... is for the courts to decide. It will obviously use the normal meaning in the English language, using a text book such as the 'Oxford English Dictionary'. These are real words which have meanings ... The word 'real' has to mean that there is a real possibility, in the same way, for example, that the word 'slight' would subtract the meaning if it were put next to 'possibility'. Anyone with imagination could think of something that were possible, but the word 'real' — in the ordinary use of the English language — qualifies possibility. Anybody applying those words would have to say that it was not an artificial, remote or slight possibility, but that it was a possibility that could result in the appeal being upheld.

INVESTIGATIVE POWERS

Sections 17–21 of the Criminal Appeal Act 1995 give the Commission far-reaching powers to assist with the investigation of miscarriages of justice.

It is vital that defence lawyers understand the scope of the powers and take every opportunity to encourage the Commission to use them in appropriate cases. The Commission should be mindful of the costs and resources involved in any investigation, and should weigh them carefully against the possibility of achieving a definite result or likely benefit.

In addition, the Commission has the power to engage experts to advise on the technical aspects of a case. The Commission has shown itself willing to appoint an officer from an outside police force to investigate a case. Clearly this approach is both necessary and welcomed.

The Commission has indicated that it intends to keep applicants informed of the progress of the investigation at appropriate intervals.

Other Factors

Section 14(2), Criminal Appeal Act 1995, provides that, in considering whether to make a reference, the Commission is to have regard to any application or representations made to it by or on behalf of the person to whom the reference relates, any other representations made to it, and any other matters which appear to the Commission to be relevant.

REFERRAL DECISION

If the Commission decides to make a reference to the Crown Court, it must give to the court a statement of its reasons for making the reference. A copy of such statement must also be served on all parties likely to be a party to the court proceedings. Clearly this includes the applicant (s. 14(4)).

If the Commission decides not to make a reference, it must give a statement of the reasons for its decision to the person who made the application (s. 14(6)).

Fresh applications can be made to the Commission at any time.

EFFECT OF REFERRAL

If the Commission decides to refer a matter to the Crown Court, it proceeds in the same way as it would if the matter had been appealed in the ordinary manner. However, the Crown Court on an appeal against sentence cannot impose a greater sentence than the one originally imposed by the magistrates' court.

A NEW BEGINNING?

It is too early to evaluate the Commission's work; however, the approach of the Commission to its task has been welcomed by practitioners. The Commission has been seen to welcome its new role, and distance itself from its predecessor. Speaking at the Law Society Annual Conference in 1997, Commission member Karamjit Singh said:

> The Commission recognises that defence solicitors have a key role to play in its consideration of suspected miscarriages of justice. Many of them take on heavy workloads, often at no charge, for applicants who are fighting to prove their innocence in the face of obstacles ranging from lack of access to material connected with their conviction to problems with literacy.
>
> Since the Commission started dealing with casework in April this year, our aim has been to establish an open and continuous dialogue with defence solicitors. There have been several visits to and from the Commission to discuss clients' cases and give updates on the progress of our investigations. Both I and my colleagues welcome the contact.
>
> We are a new body, and I want to take the opportunity today to emphasise that there is no comparison between our role and that of the prosecuting authorities. Defence solicitors should not look at us in the same light.
>
> It is the Commission's role to consider impartially all the factors that are relevant to deciding whether a specific application should be referred back to the Court of Appeal. That includes not only considering those matters which have been identified by the applicants and their representatives, but any others which appear relevant to us.
>
> We have been given wide-ranging powers to conduct reviews. We can appoint investigating officers and arrange for inquiries to be undertaken by a police officer or any other suitably qualified person. We can obtain material from public bodies and commission expert opinions and reports. We can begin new investigations into applications and carry out our own interviews and site visits.
>
> The Commission is not here to act as an agent for the defence or the prosecution. Our role is to investigate suspected miscarriages of justice, and more generally, to draw attention to related issues by means of our Annual Report and other channels.
>
> We welcome any suggestions or comments about our service delivery, and look forward to developing our communications with defence solicitors as part of our efforts to ensure that the Commission and the quality of its casework are seen as second to none.

The results will of course speak for themselves in the years to come.

Crime — Advice & Assistance

1.4.5 Should an extension be allowed where solicitors say there has been a miscarriage of justice?

1.4.5.1 The Criminal Cases Review Commission has the power to refer cases back to the Court of Appeal under the Criminal Appeals Act 1995, where it considers that there is a real possibility that a conviction, verdict, finding or sentence would not be upheld. The Commission's role is to review and investigate suspected miscarriages of justice, and to determine in each case whether or not a referral to the Court of Appeal is appropriate.

1.4.5.2 In most cases, the solicitor considering the making of the application to the Commission will not be the solicitor who handled the defence preparation work/trial. In order that the convicted defendant can be given advice on the possibility and merits of the application, it is likely to be necessary for the new solicitor to obtain and consider a transcript of the judge's summing up (in Crown Court cases) and the defence solicitor's file of papers.

1.4.5.3 These cases will often involve novel or unusual kinds of evidence. Some investigation may be necessary on behalf of the convicted defendant before any application is made, possibly including further forensic testing, the obtaining of witness statements and counsel's opinion. If an application is to be made to the Commission, then the solicitor will be involved in gathering and rationalising the material, preparing a chronology of events, and preparing the submission of any legal arguments required.

1.4.5.4 The solicitor is also likely to need to advise and assist the convicted defendant after the application is submitted to the Commission by assisting the Commission with specific queries, making further submissions (if appropriate) arising from material disclosed by the Commission in the course of the review and investigation, liaising with the Commission as to its approach and progress and advising the client in relation to any decisions made by the Commission in the case. It may be necessary for the solicitor to meet the Commission's representatives on more than one occasion in a complex case.

1.4.5.5 It may be necessary to allow more than **10 hours (100 units)** depending on the individual circumstances of the case. There is no other form of legal aid available for this type of work, although the Commission will, in considering the application, make what further enquiries it considers appropriate to enable it to investigate the case and reach a decision. It is suggested that cases of this nature should be referred up to a solicitor/senior member of staff.

(Extract from *Guidance: Exercise of Devolved Powers*, provided by the Legal Aid Board.)

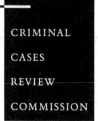

CRIMINAL

CASES

REVIEW

COMMISSION

Application

This form is for anyone who wants us to review a conviction or sentence that they think is wrong. We have written the form as though the person who was convicted is going to fill it in, but anyone can do this for them.

If you use the form, you will help us to get on with reviewing your case as soon as we can. We use it as a checklist for gathering information. Please answer all of the questions if you possibly can.

Important

We deal with **criminal** cases from England, Wales, and Northern Ireland if:

- there has already been an appeal (or leave to appeal has been refused); and

- there is some new factor which the courts have not considered before; or

- there are 'exceptional circumstances'.

This means that we cannot deal with civil or military court cases. Our information pack explains our powers more fully. If you do not already have a pack, you can get one from the address shown below.

If you have a solicitor who is dealing with your case, it would be a good idea to get help with this application. Our information pack contains a sheet explaining that you may have a right to free advice and help from a solicitor.

If you need any help filling in this form, please contact us. When you have filled it in, please send it to us at:

Crystal Mark

Clarity approved by Plain English Campaign

Criminal Cases Review Commission
Alpha Tower, Suffolk Street Queensway, Birmingham B1 1TT.
Phone: 0121 633 1800 Fax: 0121 633 1823 or 0121 633 1804

We will write to you straight away to tell you that the form has arrived, and we will regularly keep you up to date with progress.

Part 1A What we need to know about you

(If you are filling this in for someone else, please give that person's details here and your own details in the lower half of this section in Part 1B.)

Surname

First names

If you were using a different name at any stage during your case, please give that name here.

Date of birth

day / month / year

Are you:

male?   female?

If you are in prison, what is your prison number?

What is the name of the prison?

What is your automatic release date?

day / month / year

What is your parole eligibility date?

day / month / year

Your address and postcode (This should be the address you would like us to use when we write to you.)

Postcode _____   Phone _____

Part 1B

Details of anyone representing you or helping you with your application
(This could be a solicitor, a campaigning organisation, a journalist, a relative or friend.)

Name

Address

Postcode _____

Phone _____   Fax _____

Is it all right for us to discuss your case with this person?   Yes   No

Part 2   What we need to know about the case you would like us to review

In which court did your trial take place?

[   ]

Was this a:

crown court? [   ]   magistrates' court? [   ]

What was the date of your trial?   [day / month / year]

What was your crown court number or case number?   [   ]

If you were accused with anyone else (co-accused), what were their names?

[   ]

What were the offences that you were tried for, and what was the result for each one?

Offence	How did you plead in court? (Please tick)		Sentence	Do you want us to review your conviction or your sentence? (Please tick one or both, whichever applies)	
	Guilty	Not guilty		Conviction	Sentence

This table will not be suitable for every case. If you have trouble filling it in, please use the space below to explain why.

[   ]

Part 3 — What we need to know about your appeal

Have you asked a court to hear your appeal? Yes ☐ No ☐

If you did try to appeal, were you granted leave to appeal? Yes ☐ No ☐

If **No**, please give the date that you were refused leave to appeal: day / month / year

If **Yes**, please give the date of your appeal: day / month / year

Did you appeal against: conviction? ☐ sentence? ☐ both? ☐

What was the outcome of your appeal?

If you know the reference number that the court gave you for your appeal, please give it.

Have you ever asked the Home Office to consider your case? Yes ☐ No ☐

If **Yes**, can you give us the date and the reference number?

If you have not appealed, we might still be able to consider your case in some circumstances. Please say below **why** you have not appealed.

Part 4 — What we need to know about your application to us

Remember that in most cases we have to find something **new** about your case. This must be something that has not been considered by any of the courts so far.

Please use this page to tell us what you think went wrong and what is new about your case. Add extra sheets if you need to.

(If there is nothing new, but you think there are 'exceptional circumstances' that we should know about, go to part 5.)

_____

Part 5   'Exceptional circumstances'

Usually we cannot take on your case if:

- you have not appealed;
- you have not asked a court for leave to appeal; and
- there are no new arguments or evidence.

In exceptional circumstances, we may be able to deal with your case if you have not met these conditions. Here are some examples which we have thought of as 'exceptional circumstances':

- Scientific knowledge has changed, and this casts doubt on expert evidence given at your trial.
- Co-defendants' cases have already been referred to an appeal court for reasons that affect your case.
- You were prevented from appealing by serious threats against you or your family.
- Only our special powers of investigation can uncover the new evidence you need.

Please use this space to tell us:

- what the circumstances are in your case; and
- what you can show us to support what you say.

Part 6   Personal circumstances

Are there any factors about your personal circumstances, for example, your health or the health of others involved in your case, that you think we should know about? If so, please give us brief details here.

Part 7   Papers we would like you to send us (if you can)

Before we can understand your case fully, we will need to see some of the papers from earlier on in your case. If you do not have them, we may be able to get them.

Here is a list of some papers that might help us at this early stage. Please tick any you are sending with this application and put down how many pages of each sort there are. We can then be sure that they have all arrived safely.

Title of document	Tick if you have enclosed them	Number of pages
Police custody record		
Charge sheets		
Prosecution statements and exhibits		
Prosecution unused material		
Defence statements and exhibits		
Defence brief to counsel		
Advice from defence lawyers		
Expert witness reports		
Copy of what was said at the trial or summing-up		
Advice on appeal		
Grounds of appeal		
Single judge's decision on leave to appeal		
Court of Appeal judgement		

Please list any other documents you are sending with this form.

Document	Number of pages

Part 8   Authorisation

(We would need you to sign this part if we have to go to any lawyers who have acted for you during this case, to show them that it is all right for us to see their file about you.)

I want the Criminal Cases Review Commission to look at my case.

I know that this will mean collecting information about me, and I agree that they can get papers about this case from any solicitors who have acted for me in the past.

Your signature [   ]   Date [day / month / year]

Who is the solicitor who has most of your defence papers?

Name

Address

_____   Postcode _____

Phone _____   Fax _____

Is it all right for us to discuss your case with this person?   Yes [ ]   No [ ]

Part 9   Equal opportunities

We want to know whether people are being treated differently because of their race, colour, or ethnic origin. Please help us by ticking the box which describes you best.

[ ] White   [ ] Black Caribbean   [ ] Black African

[ ] Black other, please give details _____

[ ] Indian   [ ] Pakistani   [ ] Bangladeshi

[ ] Chinese   [ ] Irish

[ ] Other, please give details _____

March 98/3

PAYING A SOLICITOR TO HELP WITH YOUR APPLICATION

You do not have to use a solicitor when applying to the Commission, but it may help the Commission to get to the point of making a decision more quickly.

Legal Advice and Assistance (formerly the 'Green Form Scheme')

If you are in prison, or have low capital and low income, or you are on benefits, you may be able to get help from the Legal Advice and Assistance scheme. There is a simple application form to complete which requires details of your finances. Any solicitor can get you a form, but usually the solicitor must be with you when you fill it in.

You may have filled one of these forms in before, near the beginning of your case. The form covers two hours of solicitor's time but more can be allowed to cover an application to the Commission.

If you do not qualify for Legal Advice and Assistance, or Legal Aid.

There is no other way of getting help from the Legal Aid Scheme for the costs of a lawyer. Any solicitor you contact should tell you ahead of time roughly how much you are going to be charged, and should keep you up to date with what you are spending. Many agree to accept monthly or weekly payments. If your application is successful, you will usually be granted Legal Aid to cover the cost of the actual hearing at the Court of Appeal.

Further notes for legal representatives

Extract from "Crime - Advice & Assistance 1.4.5. in the Guidance: Exercise of Devolved Powers".

"These cases will often involve novel or unusual kinds of evidence. Some investigation may be necessary on behalf of the convicted defendant before any application is made, possibly including further forensic testing, the obtaining of witness statements and counsel's opinion. If an application is to be made to the Commission, then the solicitor will be involved in gathering and rationalising the material, preparing a chronology of events, and preparing the submission of any legal arguments required.

The solicitor is also likely to need to advise and assist the convicted defendant after the application is submitted to the Commission by assisting the Commission with specific queries, making further submissions (if appropriate) arising from material disclosed by the Commission in the course of the review and investigation, liaising with the Commission as to its approach and progress and advising the client in relation to any decisions made by the Commission in the case.

It may be necessary for the solicitor to meet the Commission's representatives on more than one occasion in a complex case.

It may be necessary to allow more than 10 hours (100 units) depending on the individual circumstances of the case. There is no other form of legal aid available for this type of work although the Commission will, in considering the application, make what further enquiries it considers appropriate to enable it to investigate the case and reach a decision. It is suggested that cases of this nature should be referred up to a solicitor/senior member of staff".

If your client is transferring instructions to your firm from another solicitor, you will need to check the legal advice and assistance position. If six months have passed since the last claim, you can always have a new form signed (Legal Aid Handbook para 2.20). If less than six months has passed, you will need to read para 2.21 of the Handbook and then write to the area office, unless it is clear that the previous advice and assistance given did not relate to an application to the Commission. The Legal Aid Board accepts that an application to the Commission is separate from advice and assistance given previously in respect of the case itself, including any other appeal (Legal Aid Handbook para 2.18 (e)).

If your client is far from your office, perhaps in a distant prison, you can use the special arrangements for franchises (if you have them) to send the application form through the post for signature. Otherwise you should read para 2.12 of the Handbook about a friend or relative of your client signing the form instead. Failing that, a member of your staff may be able to sign with the client's authority.

14   Tainted Acquittals

INTRODUCTION

As a general rule, once a person has been acquitted, they cannot be tried for the same offence again (consider, however, the situation where the prosecutor successfully appeals by way of case stated and the matter is remitted for reconsideration). For a thorough analysis of the doctrine of autrefois acquit, see *Archbold* (1999), at para 4–116. Following a recommendation of the Royal Commission on Criminal Justice, the Government made provision within the Criminal Procedure and Investigations Act 1996, for the retrial of offenders where a person has been convicted of an administration of justice offence involving interference with or intimidation of a juror or witness (or potential witness) in proceedings which led to the acquittal, and there is a real possibility that but for the interference or intimidation, the acquitted person would not have been acquitted. The Act covers acquittals in both magistrates' courts and the Crown Court.

PROVISIONS

Criminal Procedure and Investigations Act 1996, ss. 54–56:

Acquittals tainted by intimidation, etc
54(1)   This section applies where—
    (a)   a person has been acquitted of an offence, and
    (b)   a person has been convicted of an administration of justice offence involving interference with or intimidation of a juror or a witness (or potential witness) in any proceedings which led to the acquittal.
    (2)   Where it appears to the court before which the person was convicted that—

(a)   there is a real possibility that, but for the interference or intimidation, the acquitted person would not have been acquitted, and

(b)   subsection (5) does not apply,

the court shall certify that it so appears.

(3)   Where a court certifies under subsection (2) an application may be made to the High Court for an order quashing the acquittal, and the Court shall make the order if (but shall not do so unless) the four conditions in section 55 are satisfied.

(4)   Where an order is made under subsection (3) proceedings may be taken against the acquitted person for the offence of which he was acquitted.

(5)   This subsection applies if, because of lapse of time or for any other reason, it would be contrary to the interests of justice to take proceedings against the acquitted person for the offence of which he was acquitted.

(6)   For the purposes of this section the following offences are administration of justice offences—

(a)   the offence of perverting the course of justice;

(b)   the offence under section 51(1) of the Criminal Justice and Public Order Act 1994 (intimidation etc of witnesses, jurors and others);

(c)   an offence of aiding, abetting, counselling, procuring, suborning or inciting another person to commit an offence under section 1 of the Perjury Act 1911.

(7)   This section applies in relation to acquittals in respect of offences alleged to be committed on or after the appointed day.

(8)   The reference in subsection (7) to the appointed day is to such day as is appointed for the purposes of this section by the Secretary of State by order.

Conditions for making order

55(1)   The first condition is that it appears to the High Court likely that, but for the interference or intimidation, the acquitted person would not have been acquitted.

(2)   The second condition is that it does not appear to the Court that, because of lapse of time or for any other reason, it would be contrary to the interests of justice to take proceedings against the acquitted person for the offence of which he was acquitted.

(3)   The third condition is that it appears to the Court that the acquitted person has been given a reasonable opportunity to make written representations to the Court.

(4)   The fourth condition is that it appears to the Court that the conviction for the administration of justice offence will stand.

(5)   In applying subsection (4) the Court shall—

(a)   take into account all the information before it, but

(b)   ignore the possibility of new factors coming to light.

(6)   Accordingly, the fourth condition has the effect that the Court shall not make an order under section 54(3) if (for instance) it appears to the Court that any time allowed for giving notice of appeal has not expired or that an appeal is pending.

Time limits for proceedings

56(1)   Where—

(a)   an order is made under section 54(3) quashing an acquittal,

(b)   by virtue of section 54(4) it is proposed to take proceedings against the acquitted person for the offence of which he was acquitted, and

(c)   apart from this subsection, the effect of an enactment would be that the proceedings must be commenced before a specified period calculated by reference to the commission of the offence,

in relation to the proceedings the enactment shall have effect as if the period were instead one calculated by reference to the time the order is made under section 54(3).

(2)   Subsection (1)(c) applies; however, the enactment is expressed so that (for instance) it applies in the case of—

(a)   paragraph 10 of Schedule 2 to the Sexual Offences Act 1956 (prosecution for certain offences may not be commenced more than 12 months after offence);

(b)   section 127(1) of the Magistrates' Courts Act 1980 (magistrates' court not to try information unless it is laid within 6 months from time when offence committed);

(c)   an enactment that imposes a time limit only in certain circumstances (as where proceedings are not instituted by or with the consent of the Director of Public Prosecutions).

The statutory provisions are further supplemented by the Magistrates' Courts (Criminal Procedure and Investigations Act 1996) (Tainted Acquittals) Rules 1997, reproduced in full at the end of the chapter.

COMMENCEMENT

The provisions apply to acquittals in respect of offences alleged to be committed on or after the appointed day. That date was 15 April 1997.

OPERATION OF THE ACT

The tainted acquittal procedure is split into four stages: first an acquittal and an administration of justice offence, secondly a certification by the magistrates' court to that effect, thirdly a High Court order quashing the acquittal, and finally a retrial. The first three will be considered in turn.

STAGE ONE — THE ACQUITTAL AND ADMINISTRATION OF JUSTICE OFFENCE

• The defendant must have been acquitted of an offence; and

• a person must have been convicted of an administration of justice offence.

The first point to note is that the person convicted of the administration of justice offence need not be the defendant. This clearly covers instances where others do the defendant's bidding, even incorporating those rare cases where the defendant is unaware of the intimidation. A conviction is essential, with section 54 having no effect where, for example, the person has absconded before trial.

Section 54(6) defines what constitutes an administration of justice offence. A conspiracy to commit one of the mentioned offences will not suffice, nor is an offence of perjury sufficient.

- The aforementioned offence must involve interference with or intimidation of a juror or a witness (or potential witness), in any proceedings which led to the acquittal.

Intimidation is to be given its ordinary meaning and clearly includes threats. The inclusion of the term 'interference' covers situations including bribery, deceit, or other forms of encouragement.

STAGE TWO — CERTIFICATION BY THE COURT

With an acquittal and an administration of justice offence, it now falls upon the court to decide the second stage of the proceedings. Two factors fall to be considered by the court before which the person was convicted (of the administration of justice offence):

- First, there is a real possibility that, but for the interference or intimidation, the acquitted person would not have been acquitted.

This wording envisages a causal connection between the administration of justice offence and the acquittal. The court trying the former will not always have knowledge of the latter and will need to take care to establish a sound evidential basis. For example, how important was the evidence of the witnesses to the proceedings? Prosecutors will need to be alert to the need to provide full background to the original offence, and the importance of the witnesses' evidence (or potential evidence). At this stage there is no provision for the acquitted person to make representations.

It may well be the case that the acquittal was in respect of an offence tried in the Crown Court. This does not affect the court's powers to make a certification, although it may well be a factor making such an offence more suitable for trial on indictment, if mode of trial is considered.

- And secondly, that section 54(5) does not apply. Subsection 5 covers the situation where, because of lapse of time or for any other reason, it would be contrary to the interests of justice to take proceedings against the acquitted person for the offence of which he was acquitted.

Factors to be considered would include lengthy lapses of time, death of key witnesses making a retrial impossible or other factors analogous to those used by Crown prosecutors, for example that the acquitted person was now serving a lengthy custodial sentence for another offence. Presumably a finding that the acquitted person was genuinely ignorant of the intimidation may well suffice, as the double jeopardy now faced was not of their doing.

If both these conditions are satisfied then the magistrates' court must make a certification to the effect that, but for the interference with justice offence, there is a real possibility that the acquitted person would not have been acquitted.

Timing of Certification

Rule 2 of the Magistrates' Courts (Criminal Procedure and Investigations Act 1996) (Tainted Acquittals) Rules 1997 states that the certification can be made at any time following conviction (for the administration of justice offence) but is to be made *no later than*—

(a)   immediately after the court sentences or otherwise deals with that person in respect of the offence, or

(b)   where the court commits that person to the Crown Court, or remits him to another magistrates' court, to be dealt with in respect of the offence, immediately after he is so committed or remitted, as the case may be.

Form of Certification

Under rule 3 of the 1997 Rules, where a magistrates' court makes the above certification, it must be drawn up in Form TAM1 (reproduced at the end of this chapter).

Rule 4 of the 1997 Rules details the requirements of service of the certification, which at this point, maybe for the first time, involves the acquitted person being notified of the impending possibility of further proceedings. The remaining rules detail various procedures in respect of court registers and the display of certificates.

Effect of Certification

The process of certification does not of itself quash the original acquittal, it merely provides for the first stage of the process. Armed with such a certification the prosecution can begin the next stage, which is the application to the High Court for an order quashing the committal. It can be seen that the quashing of an acquittal cannot be done lightly, providing some protection against the harshness of double jeopardy.

STAGE THREE — HIGH COURT APPLICATION
TO QUASH ACQUITTAL

Section 54(3) of the Criminal Procedure and Investigations Act 1996 provides that an application can be made to the High Court for an order quashing the acquittal. The Act is silent on who can apply for an order, it would appear that any interested party could, although one would expect the Crown Prosecution Service to make the application.

The court must make the order if (but must not do so unless) the four conditions in section 55 are satisfied. Those conditions are:

● That it appears to the High Court likely that, but for the interference or intimidation, the acquitted person would not have been acquitted.

The test to be applied by the High Court is not the same as for the magistrates' court. Instead of 'a real possibility that but for . . .', the test is 'appears likely that but for the interference or intimidation . . .'.

● Secondly, that it does not appear to the court that, because of lapse of time or for any other reason, it would be contrary to the interests of justice to take proceedings against the acquitted person for the offence for which he was acquitted.

Again, it is the duty of the court to consider all the factors before deciding that it is in the interests of justice to proceed.

● Thirdly, it appears to the court that the acquitted person has been given a reasonable opportunity to make written representations to the court.

This condition has great relevance to the defence, as it is the first and indeed only opportunity to try to influence the court's decision.

● The fourth condition is that it appears to the Court that the conviction for the administration of justice offence will stand.

In considering the above, the court by virtue of section 55(5) must take into account all the information before it, but ignore the possibility of new factors coming to light. Clearly if the time limit for appeal has not expired or an appeal is pending, subsection 4 would not be satisfied (s. 55(6)).

EFFECT OF THE ORDER

Once the High Court has made the required order, a retrial can take place in respect of the original offence (s. 54(4)). Any time limits in relation to proceedings for the original offence take effect from the date of the High Court determination (s. 56). This prevents new proceedings being time barred as a result of other enactments, an effect which would otherwise defeat the legislation in many cases.

1997 No. 1055 (L. 23)

MAGISTRATES' COURTS

PROCEDURE

**The Magistrates' Courts (Criminal Procedure and
Investigations Act 1996) (Tainted Acquittals) Rules 1997**

Made	*24th March 1997*
Laid before Parliament	*24th March 1997*
Coming into force	*15th April 1997*

The Lord Chancellor, in exercise of the powers conferred upon him by section 144 of the Magistrates' Courts Act 1980(a), as extended by section 145 of that Act, and after consultation with the Rule Committee appointed under the said section 144, hereby makes the following Rules:

Citation, commencement and interpretation

1.—(1) These Rules may be cited as the Magistrates' Courts (Criminal Procedure and Investigations Act 1996) (Tainted Acquittals) Rules 1997 and shall come into force on 15th April 1997.

(2) In these Rules—

'the Act' means the Criminal Procedure and Investigations Act 1996;

'acquittal' means an acquittal (of a person of an offence) which is the subject of a certification made under section 54(2) of the Act; and

'the register' means the register kept pursuant to rule 66 of the Magistrates' Courts Rules 1981.

Time of certification

2. Where a person is convicted before a magistrates' court of an offence as referred to in section 54(1)(b) of the Act and it appears to the court that the provisions of section 54(2) of the Act are satisfied, the court shall make the certification referred to in section 54(2) at any time following conviction but no later than—

(a) immediately after the court sentences or otherwise deals with that person in respect of the offence, or

(b) where the court commits that person to the Crown Court, or remits him to another magistrates' court, to be dealt with in respect of the offence, immediately after he is so committed or remitted, as the case may be.

Form of certification

3. Where a magistrates' court makes the certification referred to in section 54(2) of the Act, the certification shall be drawn up in Form TAM 1 set out in the Schedule to these Rules, or a form to the like effect, and any reference elsewhere in these Rules to Form TAM 1 shall include a reference to such a form.

Service of a copy of Form TAM 1

4.—(1)   The clerk of a magistrates' court which makes a certification as referred to in section 54(2) of the Act shall, as soon as practicable after the drawing up of Form TAM 1, serve a copy of that form on the acquitted person referred to in the certification, on the prosecutor in the proceedings which led to the acquittal, and where the acquittal has not taken place before a magistrates' court sitting at the same place as the court which has made the certification, on—

(a)   where the acquittal has taken place before a magistrates' court, the clerk of that court, or

(b)   where the acquittal has taken place before the Crown Court, the appropriate officer of that Court.

(2)   Service as referred to in paragraph (1) above may be made by delivering the copy of Form TAM 1 to the person to be served (where that person is an individual), or by sending it by post in a letter addressed to him at his usual or last known residence or place of business in England or Wales; in the case of a company, such a letter may also be addressed to the company at its registered office in England or Wales (if it has such a registered office).

(3)   If the person to be served is acting by a solicitor, the copy of Form TAM 1 may be served by delivering it, or by sending it by post, to the solicitor's address for service.

(4)   In paragraph (3) above, 'solicitor' includes a body corporate which is recognised by the Council of the Law Society under section 9 of the Administration of Justice Act 1985 (a 'recognised body') and, in the case of a recognised body, the reference to the solicitor's address for service shall be construed as a reference to the address specified by the recognised body as its address for the purposes of the service of the copy of Form TAM 1 (including, where the person to be served is a party to the proceedings which led to the conviction referred to in Form TAM 1, an address specified for the general purposes of those proceedings), or, in the absence of such a specified address, to its registered office.

Entry in register in relation to the conviction which occasioned certification

5.   The clerk of a magistrates' court which makes a certification under section 54(2) of the Act shall enter in the register of the court, in relation to the conviction which occasioned the certification, a note of the fact that certification has been made, the date of certification, the name of the acquitted person referred to in the certification, a description of the offence of which the acquitted person has been acquitted, the date of the acquittal, and the name of the court before which the acquittal has taken place.

Entry in the register of the magistrates' court of acquittal

6.—(1)   The clerk of a magistrates' court before which an acquittal has taken place shall, as soon as practicable after receipt from the court which has made the certification under section 54(2) of the Act relating to the acquittal, of a copy of a form recording the certification (being a copy of Form TAM 1 where the certification has been made by a magistrates' court), or, where the court which has made the certification is a magistrates' court sitting at the same place as the court before which the acquittal has taken place, as soon as practicable after the making of the certification, enter in the register of the court, in relation to the acquittal, a note that the certification has been made, the date of the certification, the name of the court which has made the certification, the name of the person whose conviction occasioned the making of the certification, and a description of the offence of which that person has been convicted.

(2)   Notwithstanding rule 66(11) of the Magistrates' Courts Rules 1981, where the court which has made the certification as referred to in paragraph (1) above is not a magistrates' court sitting at the same place as the magistrates' court before which the acquittal has taken place, the entry referred to in paragraph (1) above shall be signed by the clerk of the court before which the acquittal has taken place (without prejudice to the application of rule 66(11) of the Magistrates' Courts Rules 1981 to the case where the said certification has been made by a magistrates' court sitting at the same place as the court before which the acquittal has taken place).

Display of copy certification form

7.—(1)   Where a magistrates' court makes a certification as referred to in section 54(2) of the Act, the clerk of the court shall, as soon as practicable after the drawing up of Form TAM 1, display a copy of that form at a prominent place within court premises to which place the public has access.

(2)   Where an acquittal has taken place before a magistrates' court and the court which has made the certification under section 54(2) of the Act in relation to the acquittal is not a magistrates' court sitting at the same place as the court before which the acquittal has taken place, the clerk of the last mentioned court shall, as soon as practicable after receipt from the court which has made the certification of a copy of a form recording the certification (being a copy of Form TAM 1 where the certification has been made by a magistrates' court), display a copy of that form at a prominent place within court premises to which place the public has access.

(3)   The copy of Form TAM 1 referred to in paragraph (1) above, or the copy form referred to in paragraph (2) above, shall continue to be displayed as referred to, respectively, in those paragraphs at least until the expiry of 28 days from, in the case of paragraph (1) above, the day on which the certification was made, or, in the case of paragraph (2) above, the day on which the copy form was received by the clerk of the court.

Entry in the register — decision of High Court

8.—(1)   The clerk of a magistrates' court before which an acquittal has taken place shall, on receipt from the Crown Office of the High Court of notice of an order made under section 54(3) of the Act quashing the acquittal, or of a decision not to make such an order, enter in the register of the court, in relation to the acquittal, a note of the fact that the acquittal has been quashed by the said order, or that a decision has been made not to make such an order, as the case may be.

(2)   The clerk of a magistrates' court which has made a certification under section 54(2) of the Act shall, on receipt from the Crown Office of the High Court of notice of an order made under section 54(3) of the Act quashing the acquittal referred to in the certification, or of a decision not to make such an order, enter in the register of the court, in relation to the conviction which occasioned the certification, a note that the acquittal has been quashed by the said order, or that a decision has been made not to make such an order, as the case may be.

(3)   The entries in the register referred to, respectively, in paragraphs (1) and (2) above shall be signed by the clerk of the magistrates' court in question.

Display of copy of notice received from High Court

9.—(1)   Where the clerk of a magistrates' court which has made a certification under section 54(2) of the Act, or the clerk of a magistrates' court before which an acquittal has taken place, as the case may be, receives from the Crown Office of the High Court notice of an order quashing the acquittal concerned, or notice of a decision not to make such an order, he shall, as soon as practicable after receiving the notice, display a copy of it at a prominent place within court premises to which place the public has access.

(2)   The copy notice referred to in paragraph (1) above shall continue to be displayed as referred to in that paragraph at least until the expiry of 28 days from the day on which the notice was received by the clerk of the court.

Dated 24th March 1997   Mackay of Clashfern, C.

SCHEDULE   Rule 3

Form TAM 1

(INSERT COURT NAME)

Code *(INSERT COURT CODE)*

(INSERT COURT ADDRESS)

(INSERT COURT TELEPHONE AND FAX NUMBERS)

(INSERT OPENING HOURS, CONTACT NAME/TITLE
AND OTHER USEFUL INFORMATION)

Certification of Tainted Acquittal

(insert person acquitted)   Born: *(insert date of birth)*

(insert address)

The *(insert original court)* on *(insert acquittal date)* found *(insert person acquitted)*, the acquitted person not guilty of an (certain) offence(s), namely *(insert offence details)*.

This court today (on *(insert conviction date)*) has now found *(insert name of person convicted)*, the convicted person, guilty of *(insert offence details)* being an administration of justice offence for the purposes of section 54 of the Criminal Procedure and Investigations Act 1996, involving interference with or intimidation of a juror or a witness (or potential witness) in proceedings which led to the acquittal of *(insert person acquitted)*.

This court certifies under subsection (2) of section 54 of the Criminal Procedure and Investigations Act 1996 that it appears to the Court that:

(1)   there is a real possibility that, but for the interference or intimidation involved in the offence of which *(insert person convicted)* is (was) convicted, *(insert person acquitted)* would not have been acquitted, and

(2)   subsection (5) of section 54 of the Criminal Procedure and Investigations Act 1996 does not apply.*

Date   Clerk of the Court

NOTE that where a court certifies under subsection (2) of section 54 of the Criminal Procedure and Investigations Act 1996, an application may be made to the High Court for an order quashing the acquittal. In that event, the acquitted person will be given a reasonable opportunity to make written representations to the Court.

*Subsection (5) applies if, because of lapse of time or for any other reason, it would be contrary to the interests of justice to take proceedings against the acquitted person for the offence of which he was acquitted.

To: (1) the acquitted person (2) the prosecutor in the proceedings which led to the acquittal (3) the Clerk to the Justices/appropriate officer at the court at which the person concerned was acquitted.

Form TAM 1

EXPLANATORY NOTE

(This note is not part of the Rules)

These Rules are made in connection with the provision made by sections 54 and 55 of the Criminal Procedure and Investigations Act 1996 ('the Act') for an application to be made to the High Court for an order quashing a person's acquittal of an offence. Under section 54(3) of the Act, an application may be made to the High Court for such an order where:

(a)   a person has been convicted of an administration of justice offence involving interference with or intimidation of a juror or a witness (or potential witness) in any proceedings which led to the acquittal, and

(b)   the court before which the above conviction takes place certifies (under section 54(2) of the Act) that it appears to the court that there is a real possibility that, but for the interference or intimidation, the acquitted person would not have been acquitted and that it is not contrary to the interests of justice to take proceedings against the acquitted person for the offence of which he has been acquitted.

Rule 2 provides that certification by a magistrates' court under section 54(2) of the Act shall be made at any time following the above conviction, but no later than immediately after the court sentences or otherwise deals with the convicted person in respect of the offence, or, where the court commits him to the Crown Court to be sentenced or otherwise dealt with, or remits him to another magistrates' court for that purpose, immediately after he is so committed or remitted, as the case may be. Rule 3 provides for the Form in which certification under section 54(2) of the Act is to be drawn up, and Rule 4 provides for the persons on whom a copy of the Form referred to in rule 3 is to be served, and for the manner of such service. Rule 5 provides for the making of an entry in the register of the court which has made the certification, in relation to the conviction which occasioned the certification, of details relating to the certification.

Rule 6 provides for the making of an entry in the register of a magistrates' court before which an acquittal has taken place (which acquittal is the subject of a certification under section 54(2) of the Act), in relation to the acquittal, of details relating to the certification.

Rule 7 provides for the public display of a copy of the Form referred to in rule 3 by a magistrates' court which has made a certification under section 54(2) of the Act and further provides for the public display by a magistrates' court before which an acquittal has taken place of a copy of the form of certification relating to the acquittal (being the Form referred to in rule 3 where certification is made by a magistrates' court), a copy of which is received by the clerk of the court from another court.

Rule 8 refers to the making of an order by the High Court, under section 54(3) of the Act, quashing an acquittal, or the making of a decision by the High Court not to quash an acquittal, and provides, where certification in relation to that acquittal has been made by a magistrates' court or the acquittal has taken place before a magistrates' court, for the making of an entry by the clerk of the magistrates' court before which the acquittal has taken place, or by the clerk of the magistrates' court which has made the certification relating to the acquittal, as the case may be, in the court register, of the fact that such an order or decision has been made. Rule 9 provides for the public display, by a magistrates' court, of a copy of the notice received from the High Court of such an order or decision.

By virtue of rule 1, these Rules come into force on 15th April 1997.

15   Pardon under the Royal Prerogative

INTRODUCTION

Her Majesty the Queen has the power to grant the royal prerogative of mercy to any person. It can be granted at any time, even after an unsuccessful appeal, and posthumously.

EFFECT

The pardon removes the penalty, not the conviction (*Foster* [1985] QB 115). In death penalty cases, this of course has no practical effect. It is important not to misunderstand the terminology, and recognise that the term 'free pardon' extends to nothing more than the above statement, although such a pardon could be conditional (see *Secretary of State for the Home Department, ex parte Bentley, The Times*, 8 July 1993, DC). Accordingly, only courts of law now have the power to remove a conviction.

APPLYING FOR A PARDON

Applications are made to the Home Secretary. There is no standard form for the application, and applicants are simply reminded of the need to furnish as much information as possible.

Given that the Criminal Cases Review Commission now has power to consider matters in relation to the royal prerogative, and make recommendations to the Home Secretary, it is now anticipated that most requests will be passed to the CCRC for consideration (see Chapter 13 for a discussion of the powers of the CCRC).

Index